Timeless Writings - 34

Different Authors

Tatay Jobo Elizes
Compiler
2017

Published by Tatay Jobo Elizes, Self-Publisher

This book is published and printed under the expressed permission of the various authors compiled for this purpose of making their articles and essays available to the public and promote reading among Filipinos, young and old. They own the copyrights to their writings. Authors can ask to withdraw their writings here anytime and will be edited out in next printing. Printing of this book is using the present day method of Print-On-Demand (POD) system, where prints will never run out of copies. Authors are free to republish or reprint with other publishers and printers anytime.

ISBN Codes

ISBN – 13: 978 – 1548464158   and
ISBN – 10: 1548464155

Disclaimer: Views are expressed by the authors alone. Tatay Jobo Elizes does not knowingly publish false information and may not be held liable for the views of the authors exercising their right to free expression.

Self-Publisher's Details:
Contact: job_elizes@yahoo.com
Websites: http:tinyurl.com/mj76ccq +
www.jobelizes6.wix.com/mysite

Contents

1
Reaction by Pazogie
To Jose Ma. Montelibano
article, entitled "The
unstoppable killings"

http://opinion.inquirer.net/102294/the-unstoppable-killings

Timeline: Posted at Yahoogps, Sat Mar 11, 2017

BoyM, you do great things with ideas you support. I greatly admire that in you. You've got the talent for it. You started out strongly supporting the UNJUST INHUMAN DRUG WAR and continued to fantasize its success UNTIL the humanity of the EJK victims came slowly creeping into your conscience, bothering you as it bothered everyone who had relatives killed, giving the idea that the UNJUST war has met its waterloo and had to stop on its tracks. When human rights and the clergy of the 94% God believing people stepped in, with its UN and international backing, and made its war frontally against the evil EJK, you were dumbstruck with the realization that it is a CIVIL war PDu30 was playing with no win in sight if he continues with the EJK methodology.

PDu30 and you could not listen to FVR when he offered him a friendly advice - to leave behind the 20th century and start seeing things in the 21st century spectacles. To fight an UNJUST war with 20th century barbaric methods in the 21st civilized century is a blind & deaf dog's stupid war. How can a deaf and blind win against an enemy with all senses intact?

Even Du30's loyal men are slowly rebelling at what is now a clear revolting unjust unnecessary and inhuman war, of his own making - by deceit, falsifying statistics, and lying to support his killer PNP with all his absolute powers to give them a false picture of immunity! Sowing more terror by blindly transferring erring cops to other regions to continue doing their evil via the cellphone and establishing a new turf. What foolishness! At what else does a drowning man do? Clutch anything that floats hoping it's a saving grace. From the unconstitutional Double Barrel he now wants the clergy to accompany Bato's PNP for a refurbished 2nd round of Tokhang.

Why not the clergy to accompany buy bust and arrest operations with video cams? Who is he fooling? That isn't all. Here comes the Drug Free STICKERS made from Bohol [the EJK originated from Davao. Not all evils come from Davao.

Oh, it's a terrific propaganda campaign gimmick but it is unconstitutional again! Imagine labeling a home with "This house is drug free!" What immense unconscionable idiocy! *Ay naku, po naman! Ano ba naman ito BoyM? Sige nga kaibigan, i-depensa niyo nga po ito? Blanko ako ditto, pasensya, po.TAMA NA, HUSTO NA, HINDI NA PO MAKATARUNGAN.* The unceasing RANTED FEAR has BECOME VIRULENT as you had sensed correctly! *Sus, tingnan na lang ang pagbaba ng EJK nang nagbakasyon si Tokhang at sa kanyang pagbalik? Ano ba naman?* The horrible scenario you fear did not come from the make believe scenario of a NARCO state.

Gee, look at the CORRUPTION STATE that you and I have been fighting for a long time?? THAT IS REAL, the Narco is an illusion forced by a sociopath's misplaced reckoning of where we are and putting a killing cure DDS on it where it does not belong.

On Friday, March 10, 2017 3:06 AM, J L M <jolomon777@gmail.com> wrote:

"That is the greater terror, already being experienced by 20% of Filipino families, and making the 80% fearful that they, too, would be similarly afflicted."

ooooo

2
Philippine Champion of the Environment, Gina Lopez
Fr. Shay Cullen

If you want to know the truth painful, as it is, regarding the once beautiful Philippine rain forests, the lovely valleys, the once pristine coast line, just google Philippine mining environmental destruction. Immediately you will see dozens of photographs showing the terrible environmental damage seen in the bare denuded mountains the extensive hills and valleys devoid of vegetation and left vulnerable to the typhoon rains. The water will wash millions of cubic meters of soil into the rivers and streams and poison and destroy lakes and estuaries and cause continuous landslides. Millions of tons of rocks and debris will come roaring down the hills.

As has happened already during recent typhoons, floods, landslides will entomb homes and villages and hundred more will be killed, buried in tons of mud. The rich political families behind the mining industry and their foreign investors continue to grow immensely rich and the Philippines is growing poorer by the hour as backhoes, bulldozers and dynamite gouge and pound the earth to death. Then they scoop it up and ship it unprocessed to China. The corporations are engaged in deadly open pit mining. They have not set up smelters here to create added value to the nickel and other minerals they extract.

The administration of president Rodrigo Dutere has a champion, Secretary Gina Lopez, who has taken a conscious principled stand and says no more, restore the land, halt the irresponsible mining and stop hurting the people.

She has done extensive research, made audits, and asked the mining firms to respond and explain the destruction they caused. She then issued suspension of operation orders to 23 mining firms who have failed to comply with the environmental protection rules and regulations. The corporations owned and backed by the ruling families with their relatives entrenched in the senate and congress are opposing the confirmation of Gina Lopez as Secretary of the Department of the Environment and Natural Resources (DENR).

To his credit, President Duterte has supported Gina Lopez and said to the mining industry recently, "The problem is, I saw denuded mountains, until now, the holes you have dug there are deep because it's an open pit. If that's the case, I have to support Lopez. And I cannot help you."

Duterte said, in an apparent address to the industry: "If you have something in mind about Gina Lopez, kindly rethink. And look at her passion for (protecting the environment."

It is extremely important to implement the agenda of Secretary Gina Lopez. The destruction is growing as the mining industry has expanded and is running wild after the repeal of the strict mining control law. The passing of a new law in 1995 is very beneficial to the mining corporations and their foreign partners. Lopez has said it is an unfair law and hurts people and the environment. "We have to change that," she says, adding that the 1995 law is "skewed towards the mining sector, and not towards our people."

Her concern is also for the people affected badly by the mining industry. The loss of crops, changed environment, the forced evacuations, and floods, landslides and pollution had caused much human suffering. Many thousands have been forced from their ancestral lands and domains at gunpoint.

"You cannot build an economy, a company based on suffering. I will not allow it to happen in DENR," she said. "We will never, ever do anything that will put at risk the lives of our people. Their lives are paramount. "We are an island ecosystem. It's my determination and commitment that people living in these islands should not suffer."

The Commission on Appointment, composed of senators and congressmen, has once again refused to confirm the appointment of Gina Lopez as Secretary of the DENR. San Juan City Representative and vice chairman of the CA has a brother who owns one of the biggest mining corporations in Asia.

Other government figures who have investments in mining or their friends are strongly opposed to the actions of Secretary Lopez. The ruling oligarchy makes laws that directly benefit them personally. The mining law is a classical example. They also have the positions in government to defeat and negate any true-minded and dedicated reformer. If they are challenged they make false charges against critics.

Even if the Filipinos' lands, environment, and the ancestral domains of the indigenous people are taken and destroyed, it will not stop the corrupt oligarchy, which is without an environmental conscience. The champion of the poor and the environment is Gina Lopez, worthy of all our support.

shaycullen@gmail.com, *www.preda.org*

PREDA Foundation, Inc. P.O Box 68 Olongapo City 2200 Preda Main Center Upper Kalaklan, Subic Bay Olongapo City 2200 Philippines. TO SUPPORT THE WORK OF PREDA you may freely pass on the article or republish and send a donation via mail or PAYPAL at our website http://www.preda.org *or through the Columban Missionary Society.*

Ooooo

3
Child Brides- A Cover for Cultural Pedophilia?
Fr. Shay Cullen
24 March 2017

Since she was 11 years old, Jazell was forced to live alone with an older man of almost forty years of age. She was treated as if she was his 'wife,' living in the house with him, cooking, cleaning and constantly being sexually abused. She became pregnant at 14 like a normal wife and had a baby. Her father approved it and the community seemed to ignore it or consented to it by looking the other way.

Rosita was also 11 years old. The 45-year old man in another country also had the same urge and desire to have an 11-year old sexual partner. But to make it legitimate, he paid a dowry to the mother and father of Rosita and a piece of paper confirmed it was a "marriage arrangement" according to socio-cultural milieu and religious custom. Girls in that country are devalued and have an economic value as a "child bride." She was taken away and sexually used daily and became pregnant at 14 years old and had a baby.

The first case is clearly pedophilia and charges were filed. The second case is not. Do you agree?

According to UNICEF, as many 700 million women alive today when they were young girls were treated like Rosita. They were sexually used by older male adults many years older than them. Many were as young as 11 years old. They were called "child brides." The United Nations Convention on the Rights of the Child has declared a child to be anyone under 18 years old.

Millions of little girls around the world are forcefully paired with older men when they were as young as 11, 14 or 15 years of age. In other words so-called 'marriage' or "child bride-taking" is just a cover for gross indecent criminal pedophilia. It's a front to justify child sex and escape the penalty of laws that forbid it. Most of the little girls were then raped in the act of consummation of the so-called marriage. This is one view in regard to child brides; others disagree.

Among women between the ages of 20 to 24 worldwide, one in four are forced into such relationships as a child bride. It cannot be marriage in the moral sense because clear knowledge, free consent and informed choice have to be present for such a union to be valid. But while laws are in place to forbid child marriages in most developing countries they are generally ignored and the practice is widespread.

In Bangladesh for example, 71 percent of girls in rural areas are "married" before they are 18 years old compared to 54 percent in urban areas. The percentage of girls forced into such relationships in Bangladesh for example with older men before the age of 15 years is 18 percent, one of the highest rates in the world. These old men want sex with children some only nine years old. What is the mentality, sexual urges and condition of these old men but a psychiatric phenomenon and surely a diagnosed mental disorder which is pedophilia.

A piece of paper saying it is "marriage" makes it all legal and right. But it is not all right for the child. The child suffers brutal sex abuse and a loss of childhood, education and a life of human dignity. She is reduced to the sex slave status of young girls in many developing countries. It seems the male dominated culture and religious mores are created by pedophiles to satisfy their sexual demands and desires. Such cultural and religious practices have to be outlawed and the laws implemented.

In Bangladesh the new law signed by the President last 11 March 2017 forbids marriage of adults and children. But there is a built in loophole that will still allow adults to marry children. It says adult–child marriage is forbidden except in "special cases." The law does not say what those special cases are. So the pedophilia under the guise of so-called marriage by approved laws can still go on.

Poverty is the driving force behind many forced child brides. Poor parents see their girl child as of lower status than boys and an economic benefit if they can sell her a "dowry" in so-called 'marriage.' It is income and the child is actually sold, it's a form of human trafficking. They are seen as chattels, the property of the parents to do as they please even sold. The younger she is the more she earns for the family. The pain of being deprived a normal childhood, education, separated from their parents, their brothers and sisters, and made work. It is a terrible life experience of abuse. Cultural and religious practice it seems is designed to be a front to protect the arranged pedophilia.

Some say it is not pedophilia if the man has sex with a nine year old provided it is approved by socio-cultural or religious custom. They say the child marriage phenomenon is driven by socio-cultural forces and economic considerations.

One international NGO says, "One aspect that clearly distinguishes child marriage from pedophilia is that the socio-cultural milieu, where child marriage is practiced, condones, and in many cases, perpetuates the practice . . . This is the reason, unlike pedophilia, child marriage is practiced and defended by not only the parents, but also their community and leaders."

In the Philippines where child abuse and child marriage is strictly enforced, only two percent of children are forced into a "marriage union," called that to justify the pedophilia, apparently at times condoned by the local official. Some NGOs will challenge this practice. It is not widespread yet the live-in relationship or the sex-slave union is common but not called marriage.

The child victim is left helpless and abused by a live-in partner with the consent of the relatives and mother in some cases. He provides money for the family. There is also the "areglo" system of payoffs where it is custom for some local officials, for a fee, to arrange a financial compensation between the child sexual abuser and the parents of the child. No legal complaint is filed and he gets away with the abuse and the community remains silent and condones it.

Just a few brave people will report child sexual abuse where in fact it is a common community crime and as many as one in three girls as young as eight years old are victims of sexual abuse. Many such victims have been brought to the Preda child therapeutic care center. So what is the difference between pedophilia when the same sexual abuse is covered by a so-called marriage paper?

Margaret Capelazo, CARE Canada's gender equality adviser says "there are absolutely no links between child, early and forced marriage and pedophilia." She contends that child marriage "is caused by social rules and biases that devalue girls, and related social and economic pressure. Pedophilia is a psychiatric phenomenon and a diagnosed mental disorder."

With all due respect to Margaret, it appears older men entering into a sex union with an 11 year old child is more like pedophilia than "marriage." The marriage is a front, a cultural arrangement made by men to have their way and pleasure by sexually abusing children without the penalty of the law. To save children from such grave sexual abuse, we have to campaign against child brides and expose it for what it is- legalized, economic, socio-cultural pedophilia.

shaycullen@preda.org

ooooo

4
Who Allows Cyber Child Porn in the Philippines?
Fr. Shay Cullen
30 March 2017

Thousands of Filipino children and hundreds of thousands worldwide are sexually traumatized and abused by the fast money-making crime of cyber-sex. This is the most obnoxious crime against helpless, vulnerable children. Filipino kids as young as five or six years are abused for the satisfaction of men of all nationalities that pay to see the children being sexually abused over the Internet.

Others buy videos and images of the abused victims. It is allowed to happen by the failure of the Philippine government and the corporate world of the Philippine Internet Server Providers (ISPs) since the passing of the anti-child pornography law in 2009 otherwise known as RA 9775.

Recently, Philippine DSWD Assistant Secretary Lorraine Badoy posted a sarcastic comment on Facebook that EU citizens should watch child pornography, saying in effect the people of the EU are frequently viewing child porn. She was being sarcastic and facetious in addressing the critics of the president on the more than 7,000 killings of suspects in his war on drugs. She was not condoning child sexual abuse online.

"Iyong mga taga-EU, mag-online child porn muna kayo. D'yan naman kayo magaling e."

(Those in the EU, just engage in online child pornography. Since that's what you are good at.) It was an ill-advised attempt to defend President Rodrigo Duterte following criticism by EU officials in a statement condemning the war-on-drugs.

It was considered to be insensitive and inappropriate and trivializing the sexual abuse of children. DSWD Secretary Judy Taguiwalo defended Badoy, saying the issue "has been twisted out of context and sensationalized." The EU Ambassador to the Philippines Franz Jessen said on GMA-7 news, "The Issue of child pornography is extremely serious and a grave crime. It should be addressed in a serious and responsible manner." And so it should.

The incident has a good side. It has brought attention to the outrageous demand and supply of live images of Filipino children being sexually abused to order by customers worldwide.

The Assistant Secretary is only too aware of the massive demand for live streaming of images of Filipino children being sexually abused online. The blame cannot be laid solely on the door of those demanding the crime be committed so they can view it but also on the child sex abusers, the suppliers and the enablers in the Philippines. This includes the pimps and cyber criminals and traffickers and the corporate Internet Server Providers (ISPs) who by law are ordered to filter and bloc child porn images on the Internet entering their servers.

Allegedly, they refuse to obey the law and the National Telecommunication Commission (NTC) does not, it seems, enforce the law. The telephone companies are violating the law by not having these filters in place as demanded by the Anti-Child Pornography Act of 2009 otherwise known as RA 9775. They have seemingly placed themselves above it and seem to have some government officials in their pockets. In addition to the anti-child pornography law, they are also allegedly violating with impunity the Public Telecommunications Policy Act of 1995 or RA 7925 and Executive Order No. 546 issued in 1979. President Duterte ought to investigate and make a threat against them to obey the law or else. He ought to have a war against child porn and cyber-sex.

The Philippine police are all too aware that Filipinos have hundreds if not thousands of small cyber-sex dens doing the streaming and passing the images of child abuse through their server machines. They also know parents and relatives and neighbors are exposing their children, some as young as five years old, to pedophiles online that view and copy the live and videoed sexual abuse images.

This is a billion dollar global cyber-crime business- abusing children for profit. According to Senior Superintendent Gilbert Sosa, "We (the Philippines) are the origin, the source." As head of the Philippine National Police's anti-cybercrime unit, he knows the extent of the abuse of the children but the abusers and cyber-sex dens are very difficult to detect. The dens can be a shack in a slum area, or a hotel room, with an Internet connection and a laptop and camera. It can be closed down in minutes and the suspects evade arrest. Customers in countries around the world pay per view through Western Union or similar money transfer companies. It is a crime committed in thirty one of the eighty one provinces and in all major cities, Sosa said.

Older children are also victims in that these images are freely available on mobile phones and teenagers frequently view them and are easily led to sexually abuse young girls as a result. Parents have a big challenge to campaign against the flow of these terrible and shocking acts and images of abuse. Every time one is viewed, shared and broadcast, the child is abused again and again. It is a crime that is intolerable and must be opposed and the law must be strictly implemented.

Do your bit and protest against cyber-crime today.

www.preda.org - shaycullen@gmail.com

ooooo

5
The Children are the First to Die
Father Shay Cullen
06 April 2017

The children of Khan Sheikhoun were the first to suffer as the suspected nerve gas sarin, a deadly, fast-killing agent, caused the children to suffocate their damaged lungs caused racking pain. As they tried to breath with damaged lungs, they started to foam at the mouth. Twenty died horrible deaths at the last count, there may be more. By last Wednesday April 5 at least 72 people had died and over a hundred more people are struggling for life in makeshift clinics. One clinic treating the victims of the sarin attack was targeted and hit by a Syrian rocket.

Such barbaric war crimes are revolting and cry out for justice. But where are the countries with any moral values that will try and investigate and gather the evidence and bring Assad or the Russian military that are propping up his cruel torturing regime to justice? Will any one arm the rebels with weapons to defeat the death-dealing helicopters that are dropping the sarin gas on civilians?

The human suffering as a result of the chemical warfare waged by the brutal regime of Syrian President Bashar al-Assad is indeed a heinous crime against the people of Syria. He has crossed the American red line laid down by President Obama some years ago. In 2013, the Syrian regime used sarin gas and killed more than 1,300 civilians, men, women and children.

Assad and the Russians brokered a deal to avoid the US entering the war against him by surrendering what was supposed to be all his horrible chemical weapons. It is clear that he has used chlorine bombs dropped from helicopters 24 times on civilians for several years and since 2013 has on two occasions dropped sarin gas bombs on the civilians. The last sarin attack in December 2016 killed 93 people in eastern Hama and now this latest attack in Idlib. The world is just accepting this as normal and takes no actions but just condemns the attacks. He will pay no penalty now, no red line, and why is that?

Assad must be brought to justice and not be supported, aided and abetted by Iran and Russia in the crimes of his vicious military. They have denied any responsibility and blamed the rebels in Idlib for having sarin gas on hand. In other words, they gassed themselves, Assad says. Experts say that this is highly unlikely.

Assad has been described as a war criminal and he has once again crossed the US red line against the use of chemical weapons drawn by President Barak Obama in 2013 when more than 1,300 civilians were killed by a sarin gas attack in this hate-filled civil war. The war is now six year old and millions of people have fled the country. There are twenty-thousand or more dead and at least five million displaced. Once developed cities have been reduced to crumbling ruins due to the relentless air strikes by Syrian government warplanes backed by Russian military power. They have wrecked havoc and killed hundreds of civilians.

It was the threat of US intervention by Obama that caused Assad to surrender his chemical weapons, but did he give up all of them? It's clear he kept back some sarin and had lots of chlorine. President Trump blames Obama for not enforcing the red line so will Trump do so now? Will he challenge what he called a "heinous" crime by Assad and his Russian backers?

Will he make America great again and take a moral stand against the war criminal and order a punitive rocket attack perhaps on Assad's palace in Damascus? Will he arm the US backed-rebels with ground-to-air shoulder-fired missiles to take out the bomb dropping helicopters? It's highly unlikely.

That's what the US did in the rebel war against the occupying Russians in Afghanistan and the rebels shot the war planes and helicopters out of sky and defeated the Russian army. Without air power, the Syrian army and the Russians have no chance of beating the highly motivated Syrian rebels.

Trump during his campaign has said the future of Assad is a "secondary" concern and his UN representative and Secretary of State spoke favorably about Assad only a week ago and said his removal from office is off the table. He can stay on, no matter what war crimes he commits, it seems.

As a result, Assad felt he had impunity from war crimes and so he launched the latest sarin gas attack against the civilians in rebel-held territory, some observers say. And he enjoys that impunity because of the support of Russia and China. Last February 2016 they voted in the UN Security Council against a resolution that would have levied sanctions over the use of chemical weapons. No wonder Assad has ordered their use again.

So the community of nations is faced with this horrific war of endless war crimes and enormous human suffering. Most recently, President Donald Trump has said he has changed his opinion on President Assad and Syria. Many lines have been crossed with the death of the children, he said. How will this translate into action to stop chemical attacks? Anything he does to thwart President Assad, he will find the Russian bear protecting Assad and his "friend" President Vladimir Putin holding perhaps something salacious to be leaked against Trump?

The all-group negotiations in Geneva have gone nowhere and Assad is strengthening his bargaining position by intense attacks. He has no intention of making a deal. He is hell-bent to annihilate the rebels and regain total power and continue as the cruel dictator of Syria.

shaycullen@preda.org - *www.preda.org*

ooooo

6
Fighting for Justice
Fr. Shay Cullen, mssc
20 April 2017

They were only fourteen years old and intrigued with the teenage urge to know and experience everything. They fell for the bait of the trafficker. He was able to give them money and gifts and one by one he had them join a "fraternity," a group of girls whom he abused in his private house. He gave them a taste for drugs and they became dependent on him.

Then he invited his friends over and they too sexually abused the girls and he gave the girls drugs and money. It was by then no longer an experimental teenage romp but they were being commercially sexually exploited. Soon they came to depend on the money and frequently went to the house of the trafficker and stayed over for some days and were sexually exploited by customers. He made money out of them. In effect it was a private brothel.

The federal police was alerted and followed up a tip off and discovered the trafficking operation that was going on. The municipal social worker was called in during the raid of the private brothel and six girls were rescued and referred to the Preda Home for Girls. The medico-legal check up revealed that all had been sexually abused many times. The suspect is in jail and his customers are under investigation.

We can expect a counter-attack from the suspected abusers. They have vilified Preda on the internet or may make legal counter-charges and false allegations against us as happened in the past. This is normal for human rights defenders of abused children. Foreigners who are arrested or charged with child abuse are the most revengeful and post evil and baseless allegations. Some are filled with anger, hatred and desire to get revenge against us for exposing their dirty acts of human trafficking and child abuse.

When we at Preda rescue an abused child from the abuser's home or from a sex bar, some of those foreigners accused or put on trial by the authorities will file kidnapping charges. As human rights advocates, we have been charged with libel and slander. When we campaigned to end the Davao Death Squad in 1999 we were charged by the Mayor with libel. All the charges were eventually dismissed, manufactured and proven false. That is the risk we take in defending the exploited, abused victims of human trafficking.

One American suspect who made false allegations against Preda staff went to the point of falsely charging a good prosecutor. He was convicted in court of making false allegations and was sentenced to two years in jail. But by some legal maneuvering, he has not yet served the two years in jail. He may still be behind the campaign vilifying our work with manufactured allegations and working through others on the internet to get revenge. His failure to serve sentence ought to be investigated. It's time to reopen the case.

Even some of the children rescued from the traffickers are not happy to be rescued. They are dependent and have been "bonded" by debts, gifts and drugs to the trafficker. They see him or her as their "best friend" even as a sex partner. They don't want to admit they were abused by him and others and will not, at first, file a complaint against the trafficker. But that has changed.

At first they don't want to stay at the Preda Center and get help. They don't see that they need help and want to run back to their trafficker. They want to get drugs to deal with the trauma of having been found and rescued as commercially sexually exploited children. They need to cover up their shame from their parents, brothers, sisters, friends and relatives.

They did not at first accept that they were being exploited. They were friends with their trafficker and pimp and they wanted the money. Preda social workers have counseled them and took them through the reality of their lives in the emotional expression therapy. There in the padded therapy room, they released a lot of anger and pent up emotions.

They had anger to their parents for abandoning them or misunderstanding them or scolding them. They became rebellious teenagers out of control of their parents. After therapy sessions they have now calmed down. They released day after day their anger at themselves, their abusers and their parents. They have moved from the feelings stage to the thinking stage and are listening and have changed their attitude and realized their worth as person and with rights and dignity. This is a profound shift in a human person- from a willing victim to an empowered youth looking for justice.

The Preda social worker contacted their parents. They have begun family therapy with them to bring understanding, support for the girls and reconciliation. They can look forward to a brighter future and the suspect is in the jail and facing charges of human trafficking.

In another case where a father abandoned the family and then the mother abandoned the children and left them in the care of a distant relevant, the children were sexually abused. They were rescued and brought to the protection and care of the Preda Children's Home. But the accused went to get the child out to stop them from filing charges and testifying against him. The accused influenced the mother so she filed a case against Preda, a Habeas Corpus case, to get the children back into her custody. But this will not succeed and we are counseling her to care and love her children and resist the pressure of the abuser.

The fight for justice for children and for Preda goes on. Those vilifying Preda and the children, one day, will be brought to justice. May it be soon.

shaycullen@gmail.com - *www.preda.org*

ooooo

7
Long live Mother Earth!
Julia Carreon-Lagoc
Dateline, April 2017
http://www.panaynews.net/accents-long-live-mother-earth-2/

I cannot let Earth Day, April 22, pass without a tribute to Mother Earth, as precious as your own mother—to hold dear and lovingly respect. Earth Day was founded in 1970, and every year thereafter, there have been worldwide celebrations. For many, however, the comme-moration activities have amounted to short-lived concern for the environment. After a week of being Earth-friendly, it's back to the madding crowd and to a lifestyle characterized by a glut of styrofoam and plastics and other non-biodegradables. (I hope I hear you say NO because you are an environmental activist or on your way to being one. Cheers!)

In the ten years or so of sporadic writing, I have included twice in my columns The Earth's Ten Commandments in honor of Earth Day and to oblige are quest from a reader for the complete list. Here are the ten again. Am I being repetitive, nagging, badgering? Like what we always do when we feel badgered, we skip. But please, for the sake of Mother Earth, don't skip. Read, imbibe, and translate into action:

I.   You shall love and honor the earth for it blesses your life and governs your survival.

II.   You shall keep each day sacred to the earth and celebrate the turning of its seasons.

III.......You shall not hold yourself above other living things nor drive them to extinction.

IV.   You shall give thanks for your food to the creatures and the planets that nourish you.

V.   You shall limit your offspring for multitudes of people are a burden unto the earth.

VI.   You shall not kill or waste earth's riches upon weapons of war.

VII.   You shall not pursue profit at the earth's expense but strive to restore its damaged majesty.

VIII. You shall not hide from yourself or others the consequences of your actions upon the earth.

IX.   You shall not steal from future generations by impoverishing or poisoning the earth.

X.   You shall consume material goods in moderation so all may share earth's bounty.

In a relative's house is a beautifully framed Ten Commandments of Bible fame. I suggested framing and hanging, too, The Earth's Ten Commandments. Both are just as sacred—crossing the boundaries of race, creed, color, and nationality.

Of the above, I consider Commandment No. 5 of overriding importance. I always contend that if we cannot check population growth, much of our environmental activism would be to no avail. Let me quote from a previous column: "The human impact on the environment cannot be overemphasized. Think of soil erosion and landslides caused by a growing number of people who must eke out a living by felling trees, made worse by the criminal deforestation of big business. We live on fragile ecosystems that cry out halt to population explosion." Natural resources dwindle with the burgeoning population.

According to Popcom, the neat shortcut for the Commission on Population, the Philippine population will double in 35 years. That means roughly 170 million Filipinos. The result: Poverty will become so overwhelming that society will be fraught with crimes induced by an empty stomach. Thus, slowing down population growth is "a given which transcends political consider-ations," says Popcom. Massive poverty renders outdated and irrelevant the biblical decree to go forth and multiply.

Earth Day was founded for every human being to realize the imperative to maintain the health of Mother Earth right now more than ever. Time is of the essence. Her health is our health. Read, imbibe, and translate into action The Earth's Ten Commandments before we can shout with high hopes and praises: Long live Mother Earth! *juliaclagoc@yahoo.com*

=====

Julia Carreon-Lagoc was a columnist of PANAY NEWS for two decades. She pops up with Accents nowand then.

ooooo

8

The best student speech ever by Isaiah A. Lee, U.P.

via
PENMAN By Butch Dalisay
(The Philippine Star) | Updated July 11, 2016

"We often look to larger-than-life figures to celebrate honor and excellence, from Miss Universe to near-perfect-GWA graduates. I'm not saying it's wrong to do so, but I believe the first place to seek it is within ourselves," says **Isaiah Paolo A. Lee, summa cum laude.**

I thought that the commencement speech I recently gave before the University of the Philippines' College of Science graduates (excerpted here last week) was pretty good, but it was the student response given by Isaiah Paolo Lee (BS Molecular Biology and Biotechnology, summa cum laude) — known to his friends and teachers as "Pao" — that blew my socks off. (Pao acknowledges that his sister Jillian helped him along with the speech — hurray for sisters!) I later emailed Pao to say that it was the best student speech I'd ever heard, and asked him for a copy to share with my readers, so here it is, and I hope this goes viral:

My name is Isaiah Paolo Atienza Lee, and I am not your valedictorian. I am not the best, I am not the brightest, and I am here speaking to you right now because all the other summas backed out. I'm somehow supposed to talk to you about honor and excellence, so let me start with my story.

When I was in first year, I almost got kicked out because of Chem 16. I wasn't even bad at the class. I just had a habit of scribbling on my forearm during exams, which was—in hindsight, understandably — interpreted as cheating. After an unchecked exam and a lot of stress, I ended up with a diagnosis of Asperger's syndrome. On the whole, it was a less than ideal way to get psychological support and an 1.00 in Chem 16, but I didn't fail the class, I didn't get dismissed from UP, and I didn't jump off a bridge. I could have, but I didn't. That might not sound a lot like honor and excellence to you, but that's the point.

The College of Science is made up of brilliant people. We can't deny that. The College of Science is also made up of people who pretend to be engineering majors when questioned about their student numbers and people who tasted their Chem 16 unknown analysis samples out of desperation. We can't deny that either. And we all answered our exams on bluebooks that might have varied in paper quality and might have shown different scores, but they all had the same message printed on the front: University of the Philippines, 1908, Bird, Honor, Excellence.

Our valedictorian is Mao Leung. He has a weighted average of 1.0375 and a girlfriend. I do not have a weighted average of 1.0375, and most of you won't either. I'm not going to talk about who doesn't have a girlfriend, because this is supposed to be a happy occasion. Mao Leung is a great guy, but we can't all be like him, and that's okay.

Prodigies are a curse for those who need a curve on the exam to pass and a blessing for the general public; as a whole, people tend to look at the people with the best averages and pin all the country's hopes on them, leaving the rest of us to wonder what we're supposed to do. The truth people have difficulty wrangling with is that not only do we not need a messiah, messiahs cannot solve our problems. This country just needs honor and excellence from every single one of us, every single day. Whatever it is you do, do it well, and do it for the people.

Are you going into a career in science? There might be days when you have to run PCRs from 7 to 12. That's 7 in the morning to 12 midnight, by the way. Do it. There might be times that your graphs would be publication-worthy if only you could get rid of one annoying data point. Don't do it. That is honor and excellence.

Are you going into medicine despite your teachers' laments? You might end up spending most of your nights running on adrenaline and Dunkin' Donuts because you have to stay in the hospital. Stay. There might be an occasional addict suffering from a shabu overdose that you have to tie down to a stretcher because he won't stop kicking you. Treat him, and treat him again when he comes back. That is honor and excellence.

Are you going to get a girlfriend because studies first no longer applies? She might be angry at you for no easily identifiable reason. Stay calm, listen, and talk things out rationally. After an argument about taking relationship advice from some guy who was supposed to give a valedictory address, you might see a book she would like. Buy it for her. That is honor and excellence.

Are you going to be a full-time parent because you had a successful relationship? You might proudly send your child to UP only to learn that your precious iskolar ng bayan has turned into a class-cutting, DRP collecting, tuition-burning machine despite your warnings. Wake them up in the morning, give them their allowance, and support them without nagging. See to it that they march and that you get to be with them. That is honor and excellence.

Are you just thinking of going to UPTown Center for a celebratory dinner after this is done?

You might have a hard time parking because, wow, that is a lot of people. Don't hog the disabled parking spaces. You might be hungry because the ceremony was too long and parking was nigh impossible because you left the wheelchair spots alone. Be nice to your waiters. They have names. Address them by name, follow up your orders without snapping at them, and say thank you the way you would like to be thanked for doing a good job. That is honor and excellence.

Are you going to do anything at all in your life? Whatever it is, do it well, and do it for the people. Do it well if doing it well is clocking in 70 hours a week at a world-class research institution. Do it well even if doing it well is just staying awake for five more minutes to finish a chapter or a boring lecture. Do it well when it matters, and do it well even when it doesn't. And do it for the people. Do it for the people even if you don't like the people. Do it for the marginalized even when they don't appreciate it. Do it for the privileged even when they cause Katipunan traffic. Do it for the people whether the person in question is a drug addict in the emergency room or your waiter at UPTown Center or a stranger on the internet or even just yourself, because it's not about the gratitude, or the credit, or the reward, but about the people, and the work. That is honor and excellence.

The unphotogenic, non-headline-grabbing, narratively-unsupported fact is that large-scale change happens in fits and bursts and stops, and often on a scale you can't see with an electron microscope. We hold ourselves up to unreasonable standards and are subsequently disappointed most of the time, when what matters is the work we do in increments, the lab hours that we log, and the people we encounter.

You might not make your own transgenic crops, but you can disabuse your family of any erroneous notions they may have about Bt talong. You might not eradicate crime in 3 to 6 months, but you can avoid catcalling. You might not make it to the newspaper's front page, but you can make it to your mom's proud parent Facebook post.

We often look to larger-than-life figures to celebrate honor and excellence, from Miss Universe to near-perfect-GWA graduates. I'm not saying it's wrong to do so, but I believe the first place to seek it is within ourselves.

My name is Isaiah Paolo Atienza Lee. I am not the best, but I am good enough, I am not the brightest, but I am a UP graduate, and I am not your valedictorian, but I am going to tell you all to go out there and show the world what we've got.

ooooo

9
Who Sexually Abused the Children- The Case of Lillian May Zimmer
Fr. Shay Cullen
28 April 2017

Philippine child defenders are calling on the USA law enforcers within the Homeland

Security network to investigate Lillian May Thomson. She is a woman from Scotland, married a United States national and has an American passport with the name Lillian May Zimmer, 67, born 21 May 1949. She is a fugitive from Philippine law and is likely in hiding in the USA.

The concerned Philippine police and NGOs are looking for her and will bring charges of child sexual abuse against her in the USA. US Federal Law provides "extraterritorial jurisdiction" over certain sex offenses against children. Extraterritorial jurisdiction is the legal authority of the United States to prosecute criminal conduct that took place outside its borders. If there is one law that is vigorously applied and implemented, it is the extraterritorial jurisdiction and many US nationals have been arrested, tried and convicted in the USA after they fled the scene of their crimes in countries abroad.

She is to be accused and eventually charged with spreading libelous allegations about the Philippine child defenders who uncovered her alleged crimes and reported them to the Philippines senior social workers and officials. They are campaigning and requesting online detectives to find and give information as to her whereabouts that will lead to her being charged under the extraterritorial jurisdiction law and arrest.

The Philippine government social workers and federal police rescued the children from her dilapidated grass-roofed house in a remote countryside location in Subic, Zambales. They found one small helpless child tied to a plastic chair. The other four children between the ages of five and six and one six-month old baby were sexually abused as medico-legal examinations showed lacerations. They had been cruelly and sexually abused many times.

According to court documents, the children using anatomical dolls told the government social workers and therapists they were brought by Thomson (Zimmer) to parties near the beach where foreign men played with their genitals. There was no interrogation of Thomson as to the names of the men, the alleged pedophile abusers of the children. It is presumed that they came to her legal aid when she allegedly threatened to name them.

She had denied everything and writes about herself online as if she were a saint caring for poor children. An arrest warrant is still pending in the Philippines against Thomson, (Zimmer). But where is she hiding now and who are the men that the children said repeatedly sexually abused them? A US police investigation and questioning of Thomson (Zimmer) will expose them.

The fact is that Thomson was broke, heavily drinking and chain smoking living off occasional donations to her fake "orphanage" possibly from the men who gave the parties for the children and sexually abused them. If the US child protection agency will find and question Thomson (Zimmer) about the identities of the men, they may find a group of retired US Marines and US pedophiles on her list of contacts in a pedophile ring.

The present arrest warrant stems from the hostile insulting attack on the Subic municipality police officers and social worker that first went to rescue the children. Then Thomson (Zimmer) threatened to shoot them if they entered the house to rescue the children from her as they were legally mandated to. She swore and insulted them and threw a large spear at the police officers and social worker at the door.

The group withdrew and did not rescue the children on that occasion. Some two weeks later, the federal police and regional social workers of the Department of Social Welfare and Development (DSWD) came and rescued the children and arrested Thomson,(Zimmer). She was in jail for several months in Olongapo City and denied all the charges against her.

The case was dismissed on the flimsy ground that the police and government social workers had no search warrant to enter the house and rescue the children. The law is clear that they have the right to save the children from a dire abusive situation without a search warrant.

The Mail Online investigated Lillian May Zimmer (Lillian May Thomson) and alleged these men may have been the abusers. It's possible they assisted her to flee the country quickly to avoid a second case against her. Highly paid lawyers from Manila came to defend her. They amazingly persuaded a judge to dismiss the child trafficking and abuse cases against her despite overwhelming evidence against her.

A professional photographer, a frequent visitor to the house of Thomson/Zimmer, allegedly photographed the small boy naked. The boy using dolls described to government psychologists what was done to him. Zimmer, financially broke herself, mysteriously had highly paid lawyers from Manila to defend her.

Despite strong relevant evidence, little was presented and none of it convinced Judge Jose L. Bautista Jr. of the Olongapo Regional Trial Court that Thomson/ Zimmer had a case to answer and quickly dismissed the case. A few days later he announced in open court he was retiring due to health reasons.

Indeed listening to the opening statements of the prosecution listing the serious rape and sex abuse evidence would make anyone sick. But the rapid dismissal of the charges and her immediate disappearance made many more people sick. Justice for the children was not done.

However, if the US authorities that enforce the extraterritorial jurisdiction law against suspected US nationals that have been arrested and accused of child abuse when abroad will take up the case, then Lillian May Zimmer (Thomson) may have a lot of explaining to do and face prison time in the USA.

It is now the duty of the Philippine government and the non-government organizations working together and joining with US-based child protection groups, church-based and civil organizations to campaign for justice for these abused little children. It is an affront to human dignity. The adult world has a lot of catching up to do to protect children and bring their abusers to justice.

shaycullen@gmail.com - *www.preda.org*

ooooo

10
War Bells Are Ringing
Erick San Juan
Tue May 2, 2017

Mobilization of military hardwares and preparation being done by soldiers are signs that there is an impending war and in the words of Chinese Foreign Minister Wang Yi – "If war breaks out, the consequences would be unimaginable."

The reason for the ringing of alarm bells of a coming war is that major players are on the war games and the world is nervously waiting on who will hit the button and implement the "first strike policy" or will do a preemptive strike on the stubborn leader of North Korea.

The "extraordinary" mobilization of bomber aircraft was reportedly acknowledged by China's foreign ministry, giving no further details.

The general assumption is that China is taking a defensive position in case the US administration of President Donald Trump follows through on its repeated threats of carrying out pre-emptive strikes on North Korea's nuclear facilities.

Traditionally, an ally of the communist government in Pyongyang, Beijing is widely assumed to be protecting its junior partner by flexing a deterrence force against the US. China has openly urged the US not to take unilateral military action against North Korea over the latter's controversial nuclear program.

Beijing has been calling for a diplomatic solution to the crisis on the Korean Peninsula, a crisis which seems to be intensifying following a dire warning this week from US Vice President Mike Pence that the "sword is ready," which was met with reciprocal threats from North Korea that it would "reduce the US to ashes."

Despite calls for diplomacy from China, it is also clear that Beijing is becoming exasperated with North Korea, known formally as the Democratic People's Republic of Korea. China is perplexed by what it sees as the North Korean regime of Kim Jong-Un forming an "epicenter of instability" on its borders.

Earlier this month, there was even an editorial carried by Chinese state-run media warning that China might be forced to launch its own military strikes on North Korea if it comes down to the "bottom line" of preserving stability and security in the region. (Source: Finian Cunningham, Would China Strike North Korea?)

So is it going to be China against North Korea or China versus the US? Just asking.

And the tension among the key players in this war game was intensified in the exchange of words at the UN Security Council meeting wherein China always wanted to resolve the NoKor issue about nuclear missile production and testing through dialogue between US and NoKor thus stopping the US and South Korea military exercises near the Korean Peninsula in the process to ease the tension further. The use of force is not necessary when they can solve the matter through a dialogue.

As reported by Reuters that US Secretary of State Rex Tillerson was dismayed by Wang Yi's tough words is confirmed by his response – "We will not negotiate our way back to the negotiating table with North Korea, we will not reward their violations of past resolutions, we will not reward their bad behavior with talks."

Wang Yi however received strong support from his Russian ally, with Russian Deputy Foreign Minister Gennady Gatilov reported by Reuters to have addressed the UN Security Council as follows – "Russian Deputy Foreign Minister Gennady Gatilov cautioned on Friday that the use of force would be "completely unacceptable."

"The combative rhetoric coupled with reckless muscle-flexing has led to a situation where the whole world seriously is now wondering whether there's going to be a war or not," he told the council. "One ill thought out or misinterpreted step could lead to the most frightening and lamentable consequences."

Gatilov said North Korea felt threatened by regular joint U.S. and South Korean military exercises and the deployment of a U.S. aircraft carrier group to waters off the Korean peninsula.

Both China and Russia also repeated their opposition to the deployment of a U.S. anti-missile system in South Korea. Gatilov described it as a "destabilizing effort," while Wang said it damaged trust among the parties on the North Korea issue.

These arguments between Tillerson, Wang Yi and Gatilov in the UN Security Council, and the toughly worded commentary in the

People's Daily, illustrate the folly of the confrontational course the Trump administration has followed towards North Korea over the last few weeks.

Instead of isolating North Korea from China, and getting China to impose tougher sanctions on North Korea, China – exactly as I predicted – is blaming the US as much as North Korea for creating the crisis, and is not only resisting US demands for further sanctions, but is actually increasing its support for North Korea." (Source: Alexander Mercouris Editor-in-Chief at The Duran newsletter online)

The North Korea dilemma for the UN and the rest of the world is still in the process of who will be strong enough to hold its reign so as not to start a stronger provocation that may lead us all to another world war.

Although there was an analysis in the past that the next global war will start in the Korean Peninsula aggravated by alliances of the major world powers, methinks that as long as cooler heads treat the situation with utmost diplomacy and reason, humanity can still enjoy a peaceful world... for the meantime.

But many in the know are worried about the global military industrial complex top secret agenda of the war cycle. I was told that "if the program is on, sometimes you can delay it but nobody can stop it."

God forbid!

ooooo

11
When the Rule of Law Fails
Fr. Shay Cullen
5 May 2017

It was by doing the right thing and alerting the police that a person with knowledge and commitment to defending children's rights saved a 13-year-old child from possible rape and sexual abuse. The concerned person saw a 69-year-old foreign male bring a small child into a motel in Cagayan De Oro City last week.

The child, it was learned, had run away from home in Bukidnon and was living rough on the streets of Cagayan De Oro. If the social workers of the Department of Social Welfare and Development interview the child victim, they will surely learn why she ran away. It could well be that she was abused in her own home by a relative or even by her own father. Seventy percent of the children rescued by social workers, based on our experience, are sexually abused in the home and they cannot endure it and run away to escape from the abuse. So the social workers may find a case to be made against the possible abuser in Bukidnon.

The foreign suspect, a US national by the name Anthony Bruce Mallet, was arrested and is held in the Cagyan De Oro Police Station. He had to have help to find and recruit the child, to persuade her to go with him allegedly to be sexually abused. A street child is normally frightened of strangers especially foreigners. His live-in partner ought to be a suspect too and questioned also. Mallet, despite the very strong evidence against him, is still presumed innocent until proven guilty. We will trust in the honesty of the prosecutor and the judge to determine guilt.

For 80 percent of the Filipino children who are victimized by foreign pedophiles, there is a pimp involved who lures and persuades and grooms the child to do sex acts with a foreigner. Peter Scully, the Australian, an alleged notorious pedophile who sexually abused, tortured and killed a child on video and sold it abroad had a few young women pimps working for him. In televised interviews he did not deny the charges.

Mallet, if he was arrested inside a room with the child, is in direct violation of the child protection law otherwise known as Republic Act 7610. It is forbidden to be in any secluded place with a minor who is not a blood relative. It does not have to be that a sexual act occurred or even proven that the child was sexually assaulted. Before RA 7610, many police, prosecutors and judges claimed that there was no crime if the abusive act did not occur.

That meant that the police had to wait outside the door of the room until the child was raped, abused and traumatized for life before rescuing him or her and arresting the suspect. The attempted sexual abuse, like attempted robbery, or attempted homicide or murder is sufficient to charge the suspect with a crime.

In the case of Lilian May Thomson (Zimmer), another US national with an outstanding Philippine arrest warrant, the evidence showed that the children were held in a secluded place for some time and the medical evidence and the statements of the children showed the children had been sexually abused. How they were abused and by whom has yet to be answered by Thomson. She denied all charges and the case was strangely dismissed on a technicality.

The root cause of human trafficking and recruitment of children into the sex industry is the utter failure of law enforcement to recognize the law, and believe in it and implement it. However many police and local politicians issue permits to sex bars and brothels and allow it to thrive. They do not see it as a serious issue or as a "real" crime even though the law says it is. The law in the Philippines is usually what the authorities choose it to be.

The police action in the war-on-drugs is to put aside the rule of law and shoot suspects without evidence or to get or allow vigilantes to do it for payment. They do not have the moral values or commitment to the meaning of law and its enforcement. They interpret the law as they see fit. And according to them, underage sex is not a serious crime it, appears. Some police are known to operate brothels with underage children also.

The murder of a Korean businessman by a policeman within a hundred meters of the office of the chief of police in Camp Crame in Metro Manila is another example when the rule of law is violated by those sworn and paid to uphold it.

The more recent discovery of the group of innocent civilians held by police in Tondo, Manila hidden in a secret cell in the police station behind a cupboard is equally shocking. They were illegally held and would be released on payment of large sums of money, according to them. The officials of the Commission on Human Rights rescued them.

People in general give little value to children that are not their own. The street children are seen as petty criminals and expendable. The minors are not considered victims by the police if found in sex bars but are considered guilty of a crime. The corrupt police then exploit the young girls. They are threatened with criminal charges to make them do what the corrupt police want, such as giving sexual favors in some cases. The sex bar owners will have to pay a big sum of money to get them back. The authorities tend to blame the children and minors for the crimes of adults.

We have to work for a return to sanity, cleansing of the corrupt police and a return to strict honest rule of law. We are descending into uncivilized barbarity.

shaycullen@gmail.com - www.preda.org

ooooo

12
Hungry Children Behind Bars
Shay Cullen
11 May 2107

If ever you were in Metro Manila and went to visit a Bahay Pag-asa, that is a "House of Hope" where children as young as seven to 15 are incarcerated behind bars and mixed with youth up to 17 years of age, you will see that the majority of 12 year-old children look like eight years old. This is because one in every three Filipino children go hungry and are malnourished. They are stunted in growth due to lack of nourishing protein and vitamin-complete food. There are 3.4 million Filipino children that are stunted. Take the case of Jeremy. He was rescued from a Metro Manila jail and we thought he was eight years old but in fact he was about 12 years of age.

A study in 2015 discovered that 20 percent of kids under 5 years old die due to poor health services and as many as 300,000 children under five years old are found to be underweight for their age. The Philippines is ninth place in nations that have high incidents of stunted children. The rate of chronic malnutrition and stunting among Filipino children is 33.4 percent. Poor children on the street, living in the slums and in poor rural villages, suffer the most.

If this continues and poverty remains unchanged, the Philippines will have a huge percentage of children that are stunted, malnourished and mentally challenged, unable to study and learn.

The children in the jails suffer the most from hunger and neglect. Because that is what these places are- kids behind steel bars of cells. Local governments manage the jails for children and the officials think they are criminals. They are hungrier than most, hungry for food, for freedom, for respect, dignity and recognition that they are human and need to be cared for. They need to be in school and not forced to sleep on a concrete floor and be locked up all day and night and be abused and bullied. They have no exercise, sunlight, stimulation, and entertainment, reading, games or anything to occupy them.

Imagine your life in a small cell for months with twenty others bored and going slowly insane. These children can be mentally and emotionally damaged. They are innocent going in but will be of a criminal mind coming out and will grow up angry at society and without a basic education, they have no chance for a better life than on the streets as scavengers and beggars. They are told they are criminals by being locked in cells.

They need their parents but the parents do not always know they are jailed. Many more as young as nine years old will be locked up if the Philippine Congress and Senate pass a bill that reduces the minimum age of criminality liability to nine years old. That's how the adult world of leaders see innocent children- as criminals at nine years old. In fact, many a criminal sits in Congress dressed in fancy clothes and living a life of extreme luxury, corrupt and uncaring. Sixteen million people said they go hungry in this wealthy nation where they say 140 families rule the 103 million Filipinos.

The good congress people are overwhelmed and cannot change anything. When one good senator Risa Hontiveros from the Akbayan Party was reading a column written by this writer about the children in jails, she was stopped by Senator Richard Gordon who did not want the senators to hear the truth about the condition of the children in jail. He silenced and blocked the good senator from speaking. Her right to free speech violated. Senator Gordon has been named in a criminal case of crimes against humanity before the International Criminal Court together with the President for the 8000 killings so far in the war on drugs. So many Catholics support the killings. We ask if are they Christians, followers of Jesus of Nazareth? Some churches in Pampanga are hanging banners calling for a stop to the killing and the death penalty.

The authorities love to blame innocent children for the crimes of the adults. No evidence needed. The police are frequently involved in crimes themselves so they blame and arrest children. They claim they have solved the crime and get a promotion perhaps.

Every parish in the country and especially in Metro Manila ought to have a mission to their local Bahay Pag-asa or House of Hope. He made it one of the conditions by which we will be judged on the last day of our lives. (Matthew 25: 31-46) Enter the Kingdom, he said, for "I was hungry and you gave me food, I was thirsty and you gave me something to drink, I was a stranger and you welcomed me, I was naked and you gave me clothing, I was sick and you took care of me, I was in prison and you visited me.' Then the righteous will answer him, 'Lord, when was it that we saw you hungry and gave you food, or thirsty and gave you something to drink? And when was it that we saw you a stranger and welcomed you, or naked and gave you clothing? And when was it that we saw you sick or in prison and visited you?' And he will answer them, 'Truly I tell you, just as you did it to one of the least of these who are members of my family, you did it to me."

We need to find Jesus not only in Churches but in action for justice and compassion. If not, our spirit dies forever. Let's act to release the children from the jails of hopelessness and give them a new life.

shaycullen@gmail.com - *www.preda.org*

ooooo

13
Trump's Geopolitical Miscalculations
Perry Diaz
May 12, 2017

PerryScope

U.S. President Donald J. Trump.

When Donald J. Trump was campaigning for the presidency, he projected a "tough guy" image by lambasting everyone that stood on his way or anyone who disagreed with him. His forays into foreign policy were gutsy and digressed from previous administrations' diplomatic restraint in handling sensitive geopolitical issues. He shocked America's NATO allies after he suggested that he might not honor the core tenet of the military alliance. He said the U.S. "would not necessarily defend new NATO members in the Baltics in the event of Russian attack if he were elected to the White House."

On U.S.-China relations, Trump stirred a hornet's nest when he challenged the "One-China Policy" and accused China of currency manipulation and unfair trade practices. He vowed to straighten things out in Asia.

His tough stance against China gave Japan and South Korea, America's closest treaty allies, a sigh of relief. At last, they have an American president who would stand by them if attacked, unlike Trump's predecessor, former president Barack Obama, whom he criticized for appeasing China and didn't do anything to stop China's construction of artificial islands in the Spratly archipelago.

After he assumed the presidency, he must have realized that foreign policy – which he had no experience before – is a complicated and complex game of statesmanship and adroit diplomatic leadership and maneuvering. It must have been a rude awakening for him to recognize that the practice of brinkmanship is quite different from the "art of the deal," which he proudly claims to be his forte.

And to make things worse, he appointed his friend Rex Tillerson to the post of Secretary of State. With no experience in foreign policy – or government for that matter – poor Tillerson was thrown into the murky waters of geopolitics. And between him and Trump, how do you think they'd handle bullies like Vladimir Putin, Xi Jinping, and

Kim Jong-un in the world stage? They are no ordinary world leaders; they are authoritarian dictators who love to threaten the U.S. with nuclear destruction. In particular, North Korea's "Supreme Leader" Kim Jong-un seems to have rankled Trump who doesn't appear to know how to handle the unpredictable Kim.

North Korea problem

U.S. Vice President Mike Pence at the DMZ.

In an attempt to show Kim that he meant business, Trump sent Vice President Mike Pence to South Korea. In a show of grit, Pence — like Trump and Tillerson who don't have any foreign policy experience — visited the demilitarized zone (DMZ) and stared across the "no man's land" between North and South Korea, a day after North Korea's failed missile launch. He talked tough, saying, "There was a period of strategic patience [in reference to Obama's foreign policy] but the era of strategic patience is over." "All options are on the table to achieve the objectives and ensure the stability of the people of this country," he told reporters while propaganda music was continually played across from the North Korean side.

Meanwhile, Trump announced that an "armada" consisting of an aircraft carrier and several warships were on their way to the Korean Peninsula as a warning to North Korea. But a few days later, it was revealed in the media that the "armada" was moving in the opposite direction: to Australia to participate in a training exercise. In a quick attempt to undo his boo-boo, Trump ordered the "armada" to turn around and head to the Korean Peninsula.

USS Carl Vinson battle group.

But while the exercise of sending the blunt-talking vice president and deploying the "armada" to Korean waters may have achieved a "shock and awe" effect initially, it was blown away by Trump's erroneous announcement.

What happened with the "armada" may have been deemed as miscommunication between Trump and his admirals. But from a geopolitical standpoint, Trump lost credibility as Commander-in-Chief, which effectively dealt a major blow to his ability to lead the nation's military. For not getting his ducks in a row, Trump's miscalculation doesn't bode well with his relation with Asian countries, particularly the 10 members of the Association of Southeast Asian Nations (ASEAN). Most of the ASEAN members are now kowtowing to Beijing because of their perception that Trump has abandoned Obama's "Pivot to Asia" policy that has kept most of them in America's orbit.

South China Sea concessions

Ivanka Trump and her Chinese trademark.

After the recent Trump-Xi summit at Mar-a-Lago in Florida, Trump's hard-line stance against China melted like a marshmallow over a fire. After two days of negotiations, Trump declared that China was not a "currency manipulator" and decided to maintain the status quo on trade issues.

For these concessions, Trump wanted Xi to help with the North Korea problem. In return, Xi responded with his signature half-smile but made no promises. But if there was one winner during the summit, it was Trump's daughter Ivanka Trump whose three trademarks for her jewelry and spa brand were approved by China the same day she and her husband Jared Kushner sat down for dinner with Xi and Trump at the Mar-a-Lago. It's interesting to note that the Chinese trademarks requires that Ivanka's products be manufactured in China using Chinese workers, which begs the question: What happened to Trump's "America First" slogan? Or is it still the same old "Made in China" trade policies? Does it sound like another miscalculation? Indeed, the calculus doesn't add up in America's favor. Two winners emerged from the summit: Xi Jinping and Ivanka Trump.

TPP miscalculation

Trans-Pacific Partnership.

But the worst in Trump's miscalculations in Asia was his decision to pull out of the Trans-Pacific Partnership (TPP), a security and economic agreement between 12 countries led by the U.S. Seven of the member-countries hail from the Asia-Pacific: Australia, Brunei, Japan, Malaysia, New Zealand, Singapore, and Vietnam, of which four are ASEAN members (Brunei, Malaysia, Singapore, and Vietnam). Collectively, the TPP member-countries account for 40% of world trade. Ironically, it was the U.S. under the presidency of Obama who started the negotiations among the 12 countries. Unfortunately, while 11 countries ratified TPP in 2016, the U.S. Congress under Republican control failed – or refused – to ratify it in the last few months of Obama's presidency. When Trump took over, withdrawal from TPP was one of his first acts – victims of his vindictive assault on policies and programs that Obama implemented.

Following Trump's withdrawal last February, Japan (the largest remaining TPP member) said that the TPP was meaningless without the U.S. But recently, Japan's position on TPP changed. She realized that China is moving fast to fill the vacuum left by the U.S. in the Pacific Rim region. And without the U.S. the other member-countries are playing the "China card" by negotiating their own trade agreements with China. Among them are Canada and Mexico, two of the three member-countries of the North American Free Trade Agreement (NAFTA). The third member-country is the U.S. But what made Canada and Mexico nervous was Trump's threat to withdraw from NAFTA. But it was averted when the Canadian prime minister and Mexican president called Trump and talked him out of withdrawing. Needless to say, it would have been another humongous miscalculation had Trump decided to dismantle NAFTA.

Japan steps in

Japanese Prime Minister Shinzo Abe.

It finally dawned on Japanese Prime Minister Shinzo Abe that if China joins the TPP, she would end up controlling the partnership, which would make Abe play second fiddle to China. And given the current geopolitical tremors that are occurring between Japan and China over the disputed Senkaku Islands in the East China Sea, Japan is considering taking over the reins of the TPP.

Trump withdrawing from TPP.

With all of Trump's geopolitical miscalculations, he could lose America's preeminent role in world affairs. While Pax Americana has been showing cracks on it façade, the U.S. under Obama managed to contain China. But just four months into Trump's presidency, China's takeover of South China Sea is secured. With Trump making all these miscalculations, Pax Americana is on the throes of death. And taking its place would be a bipolar world order: Pax Russica in the West and Pax Sinica in the East.

(PerryDiaz@gmail.com)

Ooooo

14
The ICC Case Against Duterte
Perry Diaz
May 1, 2017

PerryScope

President Rodrigo Duterte and the International Criminal Court.

On November 17, 2016, President Rodrigo Duterte, before heading to Lima, Peru, told the media he just might order the Philippines' withdrawal from the International Criminal Court (ICC). He got the idea following Russian President Vladimir Putin's withdrawal of Russia's membership from ICC, who the day before had signed an order to formally withdraw Russia's signature from the founding statute of the ICC. He claimed that ICC was "one-sided and inefficient" and that the ICC had failed to live up to "hopes of the international community."

Russia signed the Rome Statute in 2000 that set up the ICC, the world's first permanent court that investigates genocide, war crimes, and crimes against humanity. Russia said she was unhappy with the ICC's treatment of the case on Russia's short war with Georgia in 2008, saying the ICC ignored the aggression of Georgia against civilians in South Ossetia – a pro-Russia separatist region of Georgia. But the truth of the matter is it was Russia who invaded Georgia in support of South Ossetia's secession from Georgia. Many believed that Putin's withdrawal was triggered by ICC's published report that classified the Russian annexation of Crimea as an "occupation."

Other countries that had served notice to withdraw from the ICC are Gambia, South Africa, and Burundi, who had charged that the ICC had been used "for the persecution of Africans and especially their leaders, while ignoring crimes committed by the West."

To date, the ICC has opened investigations into 10 situations in: (1) the Democratic Republic of the Congo; (2) Uganda; (3) the Central African Republic I; (4) Darfur, Sudan; (5) Kenya; (6) Libya; the (7) Côte d'Ivoire; (8) Mali; (9) the Central African Republic II; and (10) Georgia. The ICC has publicly indicted 40 people. It has issued arrest warrants for 32 individuals and summonses to eight others. Seven persons are in detention. Proceedings against 23 are ongoing: 10 are at large as fugitives, four are under arrest but not in the Court's custody, eight are at trial, and one is appealing his conviction. Proceedings against 17 have been completed: three have been convicted, one has been acquitted, six have had the charges against them dismissed, two have had the charges against them withdrawn, one has had his case declared inadmissible, and four have died before trial. *[Source: Wikipedia]*

Among them was the late dictator Muammar Gaddafi and his son Saif al-Islam Gaddafi, who were both killed in the aftermath of the Libyan revolution.

So far, four had been convicted, to wit:

Jean-Pierre Bemba Gombo.

Jean-Pierre Bemba Gombo – A politician in the Democratic Republic of the Congo. He leads the Movement for the Liberation of the Congo (MLC), a rebel group turned political party. He was elected president in 2006 and senator in 2007. On May 24, 2008, he was arrested near Brussels on the basis of an arrest warrant issued by the ICC. He was charged with two counts of crimes against humanity and three counts of war crimes. On March 21, 2016, he was convicted on these charges. On June 21, 2016, he was imprisoned on a 19-year sentence following a landmark conviction at the ICC. In September 2016, he appealed against his conviction alleging a mistrial. He awaits further sentencing for corruptly influencing witnesses through means of bribery during his trial for war crimes.

Germain Katanga.

Germain Katanga (aka Simba) – A former leader of the Patriotic Resistance Force in Ituri (FRPI) in the Democratic Republic of the Congo. On October17, 2007, the Congolese authorities surrendered him to the ICC to stand trial on six counts of war crimes and three counts of crimes against humanity. The charges include murder, sexual slavery, rape, willful killing, and directing crimes against civilians, to name a few. On March 7, 2014, the ICC convicted Katanga on five counts of war crimes and crimes against humanity as an accessory to the February 2003 massacre in the village of Bogoro. The verdict was the second-ever conviction in the 12 years of operation of the ICC. It followed the 2012 conviction of Thomas Lubanga Dyilo.

Thomas Lubanga Dyilo.

Thomas Lubanga Dyilo – A convicted war criminal from the Democratic Republic of the Congo, he was the first person ever convicted by the ICC. He led the Union of Congolese Patriots (UPC) and was a key player in the Ituri conflict. On March 17,2006, her became the fist person arrested under a warrant issued by the ICC. He was charged of "conscripting and enlisting children under the age of 15 and using them to participate actively in hostilities." On July 10, 2012, he was found guilty and sentenced to 14 years of imprisonment.

Ahmad al-Faqi al-Mahdi.

Ahmad al-Faqi al-Mahdi (aka Abu Tourab) – He was a member of Ansar Dine, a Tuareg Islamist militia in North Africa. In 2006, he pleaded guilty in the ICC for the war crime of attacking religious and historical buildings in the Malian city of Timbuktu. He was the first person convicted by the ICC for such a crime. He was sentenced to nine years in prison.

Complaint against Duterte

Sen. Leila de Lima.

Last October, Sen. Leila de Lima called for an international investigation into the country's drug war, which had left 4,000 people dead during Duterte 's first four months in office. De Lima, a former justice secretary said that the extrajudicial killings (EJKs) must end and that the ICC should investigate them.

The following month, Duterte came to the attention of the ICC. An ICC judge said she was closely monitoring Duterte's "war on drugs" for possible human rights violations.

Attorney Jude Sabio in front of the ICC building.

Last April 24, attorney Jude Sabio, a lawyer for confessed hitman Edgar Matobato, filed a 77-page criminal complaint against Duterte and at least 11 senior government officials in the International Criminal Court (ICC) in The Hague, the Netherlands. The complaint alleges that Duterte and the others were liable for murder and called for an investigation, arrest warrants, and a trial. Sabio said that Duterte "repeatedly, unchangingly and continuously" committed crimes against humanity and that under him, killing drug suspects and other criminals has become "best practice."

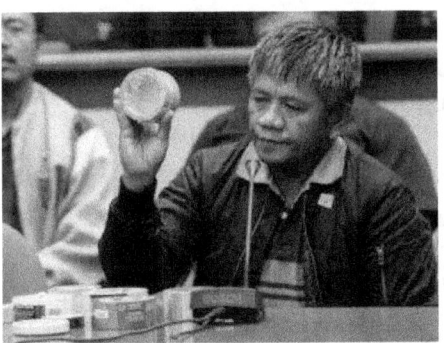

Hitman Edgar Matobato testifies before a Senate panel.

The complaint was based on the testimony of Matobato and another confessed hitman, retired policeman Arturo Lascanas, and statements from rights groups and media reports, including a recent Reuters series detailing the killings. The question is: What are the chances of convicting Duterte based on Sabio's complaint? It's not easy. And the fact that Duterte would still be president until May 2022, it would be very unlikely to bring him to trial.

The ICC'ing of Duterte

"Stop Summary Killings" rally in Manila.

Since 2002, the ICC has received over 12,000 complaints or communications, of which nine have gone to trial and six verdicts have been delivered. The ICC has no powers of enforcement, and any non-compliance has to be referred to the United Nations or the court's own oversight and legislative body, the Assembly of States Parties.

Of the six verdicts rendered by ICC, four were convicted as mentioned earlier. But it took the cooperation of their governments to bring them to justice. In the case of Duterte, it would be virtually impossible for the Philippine government to turn him over to ICC. So why even file a complaint against him?

While Duterte is safe from ICC prosecution for as long as he remains on Philippine soil, he can be served an ICC arrest warrant in another country where he may be visiting, provided that country is a signatory to the Rome Statute and would cooperate with the ICC, as in the case of Jean-Pierre Bemba Gombo.

At the end of the day, the ICC case against of Duterte, while it may seem like an exercise in futility, would bring the killings to the consciousness of the international community who can then use political pressure and economic sanctions including the freezing of foreign bank accounts of Duterte and his cohorts.

(PerryDiaz@gmail.com)

Ooooo

15
The Abuse of Children Online
Fr. Shay Cullen
18 May 2017

The arrest last April 20, 2017 of US National David Timothy Deakin in Pampanga the Philippines shows the extent of the evil lurking in the online child abuse sex trade. Deakin was abusing children allegedly on live internet streaming and he tried to erase the images when the police raided his apartment and caught him. His computer equipment was taken as evidence from which images of child abuse will be retrieved.

Thousands of foreign pedophile pay hefty fees to view live streaming through the internet of children being abused. The Philippines is said to be at the heart of the horrific trade. At any one time, as many as 750,000 child predators are online over the Internet seeking children to abuse online, according to the FBI. The United Nations describes "alarming growth of new forms of child sexual exploitation online." The FBI says it's epidemic.

The dark evil side of the Internet causes irreparable damage to thousands of young children. Their pimps are sometimes their relatives and even their mothers do it to earn money. It is one of worst faces of poverty where they sell their own children in this way. Many are desperate for money to feed the children. Irresponsible live-in partners or fathers abandon their children and their mothers. Children who are abused in the cyber-sex business or who run away to the streets are most likely to have been abused first in the home by a relative.

The anti-cyber and anti-child abuse police need all the help they can get from the public. Every person ought to realize that child sexual abuse is very common and rampart in all societies. One in three girls are victims of abuse. It is a secret and hidden crime and hard to detect as the child victims are threatened and live in fear of the abuser especially if the abuser is a relative. The child needs to be told of the danger of bad touches from anybody. If they feel uncomfortable with anyone touching them, they must be taught to run and tell it from an early age and to trust someone they can tell. They can be taught what are good touches and from whom they can receive them.

The public needs to be educated and informed about child abuse and how they can prevent it. Never to leave their child alone with a male relative for long period of time for example. Be alert and wary of friends who integrate themselves into a family and spend an inordinate amount of time with the children. Watch out for a 13-year-old boy playing constantly with children much younger than him.

The general public and government officials and school and hospital staff need to be advised of their sworn duties and responsibilities to watch out for and report abuse. They need to be motivated to report any suspicious behavior of a foreigner in any form but especially if they a see young children being brought into a hotel room or a house or to any secluded place where they suspect illegal abuse could be happening.

Riza was an 11-year old child when her mother separated with her biological father and left Riza with him. He soon began to sexually abuse her day and night until at 14 she became pregnant by him. The child was born in a rural hospital and the staff did not report the obvious signs of abuse of the pregnant child. The father even signed the birth certificate with his own name. No official action was taken by the hospital staff to report the incest. Then a neighbor in the remote village had attended a Preda awareness seminar and became increasingly suspicious of the father. She reported the case to the Preda Foundation hotline for such reports and Preda social workers responded at once.

The child was rescued and the father is on trial. Without that help from the alert neighbor, the child-mother would have suffered endless abuse and the baby would surely die. Riza, at 14, was small, stunted, underweight, malnourished and unable to care or bond with the baby. After a year of recovery and care at Preda, Riza became more caring and strong. The social workers found Diana, the mother of Riza, and reunited them. Diana welcomed the child and now cares for her while Riza is finishing her studies.

Police searching and monitoring the child porn and live streaming of children being abused are overworked and overwhelmed and are sick of the obnoxious work that they have to do and abuse images they have to view. Websites sharing the child porn must be detected, blocked and shut down immediately when they are found.

The members of the public who are sent unsolicited links to child porn website must report them and never visit the website. It is illegal to do so. They must report them to the authorities anywhere in the world they are. Child porn images are shared globally and we need a global response to combat it.

Skilled hackers who want a mission can volunteer their services to the cyber police and can with supervision be deputized to search, find and report the online abusers. Evidence can be gathered so the pedophiles and pornographers can be caught and prosecuted.

Internet Server Providers (ISP) in the Philippines are bound by law to block and filter all child porn images but they steadfastly refuse to do so, it seems. The telephone companies are violating the law by not having these filters in place as demanded by the Anti-Child Pornography Act of 2009 otherwise known as RA 9775. They have seemingly placed themselves above the law and may have some government officials in their pockets. In addition to the anti-child pornography law, they are also allegedly violating with impunity the Public Telecommunications Policy Act of 1995 or RA 7925 and Executive Order No. 546 issued in 1979.

Profits are more important to them than the well being of children, it would seem. Government officials of the National Telecommunications Commission who are duty-bound to implement the law are also inactive and ignore the violations of the law by the ISPs. Why we ask?

If this law was implemented and followed to protect children, there would less abuse of children online. The likes of Deakin and other notorious child abusers local and foreign could be brought to justice sooner. It is a collective responsibility and we have to work together to stand against the corrupt officials and the abusers and defend and protect the children.

shaycullen@gmail.com –*www.preda.org.*

ooooo

16
Did Xi Take Trump for a Ride
Perry Diaz
May 23, 2017
PerryScope

When President Donald Trump met his Chinese counterpart Xi Jinping at his luxurious resort Mar-a-Lago in Palm Beach, Florida last April 6, he was hoping that Xi would accept his invitation to stay at the posh resort. Well, Xi politely declined and instead stayed at a nearby hotel. But other than that, their summit was deemed a "success." Trump got something of geopolitical value that he thought would solve his North Korea dilemma. And Xi got something of great economic value that he coveted so much. But how do you measure who got more? It's like comparing apples and oranges, right?

After the recent Trump-Xi summit at Mar-a-Lago in Florida, Trump's hard-line stance against China melted like a marshmallow over a fire. After two days of negotiations, Trump declared that China was not a "currency manipulator" and decided to maintain the status quo on trade issues. That's a 180-degree turnaround from his position during the presidential campaign.

When Xi went back home, he ordered shipments of coal from North Korea to be turned back. Trump was ebullient when he got the news. He said that China took a "big step" in easing tensions between the two countries. He described his relationship with Xi as one with "good chemistry" and praised Xi for banning North Korean coal.

South Korea's new president Moon Jae-in and North Korean "supreme leader" Kim Jong-un.

But what has that to do with the North Korea "nuclear" problem? North Korea continues her nuclear program including developing intercontinental ballistic missiles (ICBMs) that could reach the U.S. Since the Trump-Xi summit, North Korea had attempted to launch ballistic missiles but failed when the missiles exploded in flight. The following day that South Korea elected Moon Jae-In as president, North Korea launched another missile test. It was successful. This led Moon to comment that war with North Korea was a "high possibility."

"Nuclear card"

Strategic Significance of the
SOUTH CHINA SEA

Meanwhile, the situation in the South China Sea (SCS) has drastically changed: China put militarization of the region in high gear. In an attempt to please – or appease – China, Trump isn't doing anything. He even turned down three requests from the Pacific Fleet to conduct freedom of navigation operations (FONOPs) with 12 miles of China's militarized islands in the Spratlys. And in an act of arrogance, China's ambassador to the U.S. demanded that Trump remove the Commander of the U.S. Pacific Command, Admiral Harry Harris Jr., who has been a strong proponent of FONOP. But what reportedly irked China was when Harris called China "aggressive," saying the country does not "seem to respect the international agreements they've signed." He was referring to the Permanent Court of Arbitration (PCA) ruling that rejected China's "nine-dash line" claim, which covered 80% of the SCS.

North Korea's recent test launch of new ballistic missile Hwasong-12, which North Korea claims could reach the U.S.

Evidently, Xi has put Trump on ice by playing the North Korea "nuclear card." In other words, North Korea can now pursue her nuclear program, knowing that Trump wouldn't do anything to stop her for as long as Xi pursues the "denuclearization" of the Korean Peninsula. But for North Korea watchers, denuclearization is not going to happen because China wouldn't allow it to happen. If China wanted it to happen, she could have done it long time ago.

Another thing that's not going to happen is Korean reunification. If reunification were going to happen, it would be under a democratic government and China wouldn't allow that to happen.

Indeed, a divided Korea — with North Korea possessing nuclear weapons — would serve as a security buffer between China and the U.S. forces stationed just south of the demilitarized zone (DMZ). But if the North Korean communist government collapses and the Korean Peninsula is reunified under the South Korea government, China will lose a strategic advantage over the western part of the Sea of Japan; thus, giving South Korea and Japan full control of the Sea of Japan. This would allow South Korea and Japan to block the Korea Strait – which connects the Sea of Japan and the East China Sea (ECS) – if hostility with China erupts.

Senkaku Islands.

It's important to note that ECS is a hotly disputed region between China and Japan. The dispute is about ownership of the Senkaku Islands, a group of eight uninhabited isles and islets administered by Japan but contested by China. The sea's strategic value is important to China because it connects to the SCS through the Taiwan Strait. To the east of the ECS is the Ryukyu archipelago, which is Japanese territory and to the west is China.

Arbitral tribunal

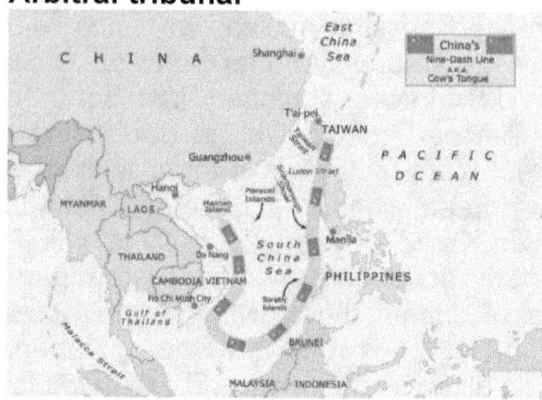

Nine-dash line.

This brings us back to the SCS, which China claims by virtue of the "nine-dash line," an arbitrary line that demarcates 80% of the South China Sea. But last July, the Permanent Court of Arbitration (PCA) in The Hague, Netherlands, issued a ruling in the Republic of the Philippines vs. People's Republic of China that invalidates the "nine-dash line," thus rendering China's claim null and void. Beijing immediately rejected the PCA's ruling.

Meanwhile, the newly elected President Rodrigo Duterte of the Philippines, who was sworn into office just 12 days prior to the PCA tribunal award, had a different idea. Instead of pursuing the PCA's award, he "temporarily" set it aside. During an event at the *Libingan ng mga Bayani* (Heroes' Cemetery), Duterte told Chinese Ambassador Zhao Jinhua that he does not want to go to war with China. Duterte then proposed that both the Philippines and China should just have a "soft landing everywhere." After Duterte's decision to set the tribunal award temporarily, China showered the Philippines with financial loans.

Rude awakening

Xi Jinping asked the PLA to be ready for a "regional war." (File Photo: September 2014).

Last May 15, Duterte met with Chinese President Xi Jinping during the "One Belt, One Road" summit in Beijing. Duterte told Xi, *"We intend to drill oil there, if it's yours, well, that's your view, but my view is I can drill the oil, if there is some inside the bowels of the earth, because it is ours."* Xi responded, saying: ***"Well, if you force this, we'll be forced to tell you the truth. We will go to war. We will fight you."***

It must have been a rude awakening for Duterte who had called Xi a "great president." "China loves the Philippines and the Filipino people," Duterte once said of his new friend and idol. Who would go to war with a friend? Clearly, things have changed, which begs the question: Why the direct and undiplomatic verbal assault on Duterte?

Xi knows that Duterte is weak – very weak – who by his own admission said *"We cannot stop China from doing its thing. What do you want me to do? Declare war against China? I can, but we'll lose all our military and policemen tomorrow!"* If Xi uses Sun Tzu's *"Art of War"* tactics, he knows that not only Duterte is weak; U.S. President Donald Trump is weak, too. And this raises the question: Would Trump honor the U.S.-Philippines Mutual Defense Treaty (MDT) if Duterte invoked it? If no, then the Philippines would be helplessly at the mercy of China. And for as long as Xi keeps promising Trump that he's working to denuclearize the Korean Peninsula, Trump would remain neutral in the territorial disputes in the SCS.

When Xi warned Duterte, "We will go to war," he knew exactly what Duterte would do: Withdraw. And if Duterte has the cojones to proceed drilling for oil, what would Xi do? Would he ask Trump to rein in Duterte just like when Trump asked Xi to rein in North Korea's "supreme leader," Kim Jong-un?

Indeed, any way it's played out, Xi wins. He keeps North Korea nuclear-armed and the South China Sea in his possession. Which makes one wonder: Did Xi take Trump for a ride when they met at Mar-a-Lago?

(PerryDiaz@gmail.com)

Ooooo

17
Trump's 'House of Cards'
Perry Diaz
May 15, 2017

PerryScope

On the day of Donald J. Trump's presidential inauguration, a trailer of Season 5 of the "House of Cards" Netflix series was shown. The trailer – which movie critics dubbed "creepy" – accompanied an upside down American flag, along with the tweet: *"We make terror."* This line is a recall of last season's final episode, when Underwood said, *"We don't submit to terror. We make the terror."*

I am not trying to promote the controversial series but I can't help but notice the stark similarities between Trump and President Francis J. Underwood, the villainous character in the "House of Cards." Sometimes it makes me wonder whether Trump is play-acting the role of the scheming and wily Underwood or Underwood is playing the real-life Trump.

It seems like the producers are going to take "House of Cards" to a level that would parallel the Trumpian presidency – with all the intrigues, lies, corruption, dirt, and warts that would make Underwood look like an altar boy. Yes, Season 5 will be all about Trump masquerading as Underwood. It would be Trump's "House of Cards."

Trump and Francis J. Underwood, plays U.S. president in the Netflix series "House of Cards."

For starters, the similarity of personality between Trump and Underwood makes people wonder if the presidency is no longer the domain of statesmen who are more concerned about policy rather than politics. Gone are the days when the nation's elected leaders brought honor to the presidency. Trump, in the first 100 days of his presidency has dragged the office to a level of disrespect not seen before. Indeed, his first acts as president created chaos, which set the tone of how he is going to run the government for the next four years.

Assault on women

Women protesting Trump's assault on women.

But if the first week of Trump's presidency was a precursor of what it would be like in the next 200 weeks, then the American people should be prepared to ride a roller coaster endlessly. Indeed, Trump did not disappoint them when the day after his inauguration, hundreds of thousands of women gathered in Washington to express their disgust over Trump's misogynistic behavior against women. In cities across the country, hundreds of thousands more converged on the streets in a show of solidarity.

Indeed, like Underwood, Trump's attitude on women smacks of the demeaning – and brutal — treatment of women during the dark ages. And this is manifested in his attempt to repeal the Affordable Care Act or "Obamacare" and replace it with a healthcare system that is deemed as an assault on women's health. With a majority of Americans expressing their opposition to *"Trumpcare,"* Trump demonstrated his cold-blooded persona by ignoring the nation's cry for compassion for the tens of millions who would be denied health coverage under Trumpcare, mostly women and the poor. Which makes one wonder:

What is the underlying reason for Trump's obsession to repeal Obamacare and replace it with his own creation?

Trumpkenstein.

His first executive order – on Inauguration Day – involved "minimizing the economic burden" of Obamacare. But if there is one thing that's has emerged in his brazen experimentation of the people's healthcare is that he has created a Frankenstein… or should I say, Trumpkenstein?

Assault on immigrants

Americans protesting Trump's assault on immigrants.

While it's bad enough that creating Trumpkenstein is awfully insensitive, Trump's assault on immigrants – particularly those who are from certain Middle East countries – is repugnant and bespeaks of his anti-immigrant and anti-Muslim sentiment, which is driven by his "white nationalist" and anti-immigration xenophobia. The fact that he hired Steve Bannon – an avowed "white nationalist" with racist predisposition – to be his senior strategist and advisor, shows his disdain for people of color. Bannon, formerly the power behind the right-wing Breitbart News website, was the author of Trump's controversial travel ban executive orders.

A week after his inauguration, Trump signed the executive order "Protecting the Nation from Foreign Terrorist Entry into the United States," the so-called "Travel Ban." However, immigration advocates call it more aptly, "Muslim Ban." When the Federal Court stopped its implementation, Trump revised it to make it more legally "palatable." But once again the Federal Court rejected it. It is now on appeal.

"Golden Visas" for sale

Jared Kushner's father Charles Kushner and sister Nicole Meyer and a rendering on One Journal Square building

they're trying to fund with the sale of "Golden Visas" to wealthy Chinese investors.

But while the travel ban restricts, if not prohibits, the issuance of visas to people from seven predominantly Muslim countries, a scandal erupted recently involving Trump's family. It was revealed in the media that Trump's senior adviser and son-in-law Jared Kushner's family real estate business, "The Kushner Companies" – which holds around 20,000 apartments and 13 million square feet of commercial space across the U.S. — is involved in promoting a program that would allow wealthy foreigners in obtaining EB-5 Investor Visas, pejoratively called "Golden Visas."

A wide screen image showing a juxtaposition of Kushner1 project and President Trump displayed behind the podium where Nicole Meyer is making a project presentation.

Recently, Jared's sister Nicole Kushner Meyer organized an event in Beijing to lure 300 wealthy Chinese to invest a total of $150 million in a 79-story apartment building in New Jersey called Kushner 1. Marketing materials distributed by Nicole cited the Kushner family's "celebrity" status. Although the White House said that Jared has no involvement in the project, the family's relationship with Trump was highlighted when a wide screen image showing a juxtaposition of the project and President Trump was displayed behind the podium. Like they say, "A picture is worth a thousand words." Yes, indeed.

Surmise it to say, if the name-dropping and showing of Trump's image on the wall was intended to attract and influence people to invest, then one can say that such ploy is tantamount to "influence peddling," which constitutes corruption. And by the way, during the marketing presentation, journalists were asked to leave the room.

Abuse of power

Trump meets Russia's Foreign Minister Sergey Lavrov (left) and Ambassador to the U.S. Sergey Kislyak (right) in the Oval Office.

Trump promised to "drain the swamp" at the nation's capital, but instead he raised the level of corruption, which has become a trademark of the Trump presidency. And then there is also the alleged collusion between the Trump campaign and Russia to hack the U.S. elections in favor of Trump, who won the presidency by garnering a majority of the Electoral College votes. However, he lost the popular vote to Hillary Clinton by more than three million votes. While this quirk in the political system had happened a few times in the past due mainly to the way the Electoral College votes were distributed, Trump's victory is being questioned by many people who blamed Russia's alleged hacking had changed the calculus of the election results.

To date, the FBI investigation into possible Trump-Russia collusion has caused heads to fall. The first was acting Attorney General Sally Yates whom Trump fired after she warned the White House about former National Security Adviser Gen. Michael Flynn's questionable contacts with some high Russian officials. Consequently, Trump fired Flynn. And then there was Congressman Jason Chaffetz, Chairman of the House Oversight and Government Reform Committee, who was torn between loyalty to the Republican Party and to his duty as "ethics watchdog." Faced with a lose-lose dilemma, he resigned from his congressional seat.

Last May 9, Trump fired FBI Director James Comey. According to Comey, he was fired because: (1) He never provided Trump with any assurance of personal loyalty, and (2) The FBI's investigation into possible Trump team collusion with Russia in the 2016 election was accelerating. And to complicate things, Deputy Attorney General Rod Rosenstein reportedly threatened to quit after he was named as the "driving force" – which he denied — behind Trump's decision to fire Comey.

There were two collateral damages to the Trump-Russia collusion investigation. The first was Attorney General Jeff Sessions who recused himself from the investigation. And the second was Congressman Devin Nunes who recused himself as Chairman of the House Intelligence Committee after he announced that he was under investigation by the House Committee on Ethics because of public reports that he "may have made unauthorized disclosures of classified information."

Angela Reid, former White House Usher fired by Trump without any explanation.

Unrelated to the Trump-Russia investigation, Trump fired another Federal employee: Angela Reid, former White House Usher. No reason was given for the firing of Reid who was a native of Jamaica. But what is glaringly apparent is that Reid is a woman, an immigrant, and a person of color! Did Trump fire her because she didn't fit into the "white nationalist" crowd that he surrounds himself with in the White House?

With all these people being fired or resigning from the government, it makes one wonder if the "House of Cards" that Trump built on lies, intrigues, and deceit would survive public scrutiny. *(PerryDiaz@gmail.com)*

Ooooo

18
"My Family's Slave," The Unpleasant Truth
Fr. Shay Cullen
26 May 2017

"My Family's Slave" is a personal story written by Filipino Alex Tizon who died last March 1, 2017 and who grew up in America when he migrated with his family. He was four years old at the time. He left behind a moving and conscience-searing true story about his "yaya" or family's "katulong," the woman who cared for him and worked her whole life for his family unpaid. Some would praise her devotion and sacrifice, Alex said it was slavery.

He wrote about this village girl from Tarlac, Eudocia Tomas Pulido, 18 years old and given as a gift to his mother by his grandfather as a house help. He was a patriarchic well-off landowning grandfather. Eudocia was a docile, submissive village girl intimidated by the powerful man and with a vague sense that her family owed something to the old man and she had a "debt of gratitude" to repay it with her whole life in servitude, That is a strong "utang-na-loob," or "debt of gratitude" that has to be satisfied and prevents a person from quitting. But it is dishonorable when the person is exploited over it.

Eudocia Tomas Pulido worked without recompense of any kind in the house of the Tizons in Tarlac. She would take beatings from the grandfather in place of her mistress. She was scolded and blamed even for resting when she was sick. When the family moved to America in the 1960s she was brought along as a " family helper," free unpaid labor. Alex wrote, "She lived with us for 56 years. She raised me and my siblings without pay. I was 11, a typical American kid, before I realized who she was."

The Tizons were considered in America as a model family, good Catholics, but as we now know, with a fragmented, unreflecting hypocritical form of "Christianity." There are millions of upright true honest Filipino families that would never do such a thing or exploit anyone but others sadly do it. Such people today are living a contradictory illusion of being Christian. Like many, they think that killing suspects without evidence or due process is a good and right action. Their conscience apparently does not bother them one bit.

The article by Alex Tizon is doing the rounds on social media and is challenging and troubling the conscience of many a family who have had similar "utusans" (those who follow orders) or "katulongs" (helpers) or "kasambahay" (domestics), many of whom would have been like Eudocia, and dare we say it, as did Alex, isang alipin, a slave. How many more helpers are held "captive" in "bonded unpaid labor," kept in the house, denied freedom, marriage, a family, pay and a home of their own.

Eudocia was property, given as a "slave" and owned by the family for them to do with her as they liked. Her few requests in her lifetime were denied. When the mother of Alex died (the father had deserted the family), Alex took her in, paid her US $200 a week and gave her her own room and all her needs and a free human life. He took her on a visit to her family in Tarlac after he got her migrant legal status properly established. But she knew no one and went back to the US with Alex.

This story uncovers the culture of exploitation in various forms of domestic slavery that is rampant in our society. The injustice of such lives of servitude is never considered. It is accepted as a cultural right of a dominant family over the weaker. It reflects a status-conscious society where possessions and wealth determine one's standing and value. It shows how easily the poor, hungry, unemployed and uneducated can be easily exploited by those above them.

The poor are generally considered by the rich as of lesser value as humans and unworthy to improve their lives. It is a challenge to the kind of Catholic Church teaching which critics have said is too sacramental, theologically abstract, impractical and unrelated to daily life. Teaching the people the strong values of compassion, justice, human dignity, and freedom and taking an active principled stand for them is rare and these values are at the heart and meaning of Christian life. Without living them daily with commitment, we are just church-going Catholics.

So with human exploitation entrenched in parts of the culture, let us not be shocked to learn that over a hundred thousand young teenage girls are coerced, tricked, groomed and lured into the Philippine sex industry every year. They are recruited by the promise of good jobs then they are cheated and exploited. It is the same old cruel story. Local officials give permits to the sex bars as a common practice so they approve and support the sex-for-sale industry and the human trafficking and exploitation.

Another kind of slavery is that imposed on many children, some as young as 10 and 12. They are sexually abused live on the Internet in cyber-sex dens. High paying customers in rich countries view their images. The law says the Internet Server Providers (ISPs) and telecommunication corporations must filter and block the child pornography and cybersex images. But they choose not to do so and some in the National Telecommunications (NTC) appears to be in collusion with them. This is a culture where the powerful say what the law is and is not.

www.preda.org - shaycullen@gmail.com

ooooo

19
Why China Will Declare War If PH Drills for Oil
Rodel Rodis
June 7, 2017

On May 19, 2017, President Rodrigo Duterte disclosed at a press conference in Manila that he met with Chinese President Xi Jinping during the "One Belt, One Road" summit in Beijing on May 15 and told Xi of his country's intention to drill for oil in the West Philippine Sea.

"We intend to drill oil there, if it's yours, well, that's your view, but my view is, I can drill the oil, if there is some inside the bowels of the earth, because it is ours," Duterte said he told Xi.

"His response to me, 'we're friends, we don't want to quarrel with you, we want to maintain the presence of warm relationship, but if you force the issue, we'll go to war," Duterte said.

https://www.youtube.com/watch?v=DSG

Xi's threat was unmistakable. This was Xi's message: "We're friends as long as you accept the fact that the South China Sea is ours, all of it including the portion you call the West Philippine Sea. As long as you accept this, we will provide you with generous loans to fund your infrastructure projects. But if you drill for oil there, we will declare war on you."

Why did Duterte disclose Xi's threat when he had been extolling the leadership of Xi and had been moving the Philippines away from the United States towards his embrace of China?

Why did Xi risk alienating his closest ally in Southeast Asia by openly threatening him with war if he asserted sovereignty over his country's territorial waters?

Xi may recall that when Duterte visited China on a state visit in October 2016, he announced his military and economic "separation" from the U.S. "America has lost now. I've realigned myself in your ideological flow. And maybe I will also go to Russia to talk to Putin and tell him that there are three of us against the world: China, Philippines and Russia. It's the only way."

Just three weeks earlier, on April 29, 2017, at the opening of the Summit of the Association of Southeast Asian Nations (ASEAN) in Manila, Duterte told reporters that the there was "no point" for ASEAN to protest Chinese artificial island building in disputed areas of the South China Sea because ASEAN was "helpless" to stop China.

"It cannot be an issue anymore. It's already there. What would be the purpose also of discussing it if you cannot do anything," Duterte said referring to China's transformation of reefs and shoals in areas of the sea claimed by the Philippines and other nations into artificial islands, and installing military facilities there.

The United States and other nations have criticized China's militarization of the waterway where $5 trillion in annual trade passes as a serious threat to freedom of navigation. China's Foreign Ministry spokeswoman Hua Chunying did not dispute the essence of the Xi-Duterte conversation but described it merely as part of their agreement to "strengthen communication" on important bilateral issues.

Duterte's new Secretary of Foreign Affairs former Sen. Alan Peter Cayetano echoed the Chinese version saying "The conversation was very frank. There was mutual respect, there was mutual trust," Cayetano told reporters even though he was not present when the conversation occurred.

"The context was not threatening each other, that we will go to war. The context is how do we stabilize the region and how do we prevent conflict," Cayetano added.

What the Chinese and Philippine foreign ministries will not answer is the question WHY.

The answer can be found in a news article that appeared on May 18, 2017 entitled "China successfully mines flammable ice from the South Sea"

http://www.mining.com/china-success...
.

"In a first for the country, engineers extracted the gas from the so-called "flammable ice" – methane hydrate, where the gas is trapped in ice crystals – and converted it to natural gas in a single, continuous operation on a floating production platform.

After nearly two decades of research and exploration, China has successfully mined so-called "flammable ice" in what authorities qualify as a major breakthrough that may lead to a global energy revolution.

The element, a kind of natural gas hydrate, was discovered in the area in 2007, but this is the first time the country is able to successfully extract combustible ice from the seabed, in a single, continuous operation on a floating production platform in the Shenhu area of the South China Sea, about 300km southeast of Hong Kong, state-run Xinhua news agency reports."

Methane hydrate global sources are estimated to exceed the combined energy content of all other fossil fuels."

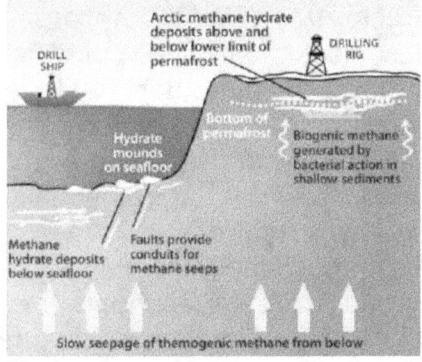

Estimates of the South China Sea's methane hydrate potential now range as high as 150 billion cubic meters of natural gas equivalent, sufficient to satisfy China's entire equivalent oil consumption for 50 years.

The commercial production of methane hydrate would reduce China's dependence on energy imports, which accounts for nearly 60% of its crude oil needs, making it the world's No. 2 importer by volume, after the U.S.

Methane hydrate will also aid China's efforts to shift to natural gas from coal, which accounts for nearly 70% of its primary-energy consumption, which has caused harmful pollution to China's cities.

China's discovery of methane hydrates off the coasts of Vietnam and the Philippines is what has prompted China to aggressively pursue the occupation of Philippine and Vietnamese shoals and their conversion to artificial islands in order to safely conduct its exploration and production of methane hydrate.

This explains China's placement of an oil rig platform off the coast of Vietnam which triggered international showdowns with Vietnam.

The Recto Bank (Reed Bank) area located only 50 miles west of the Philippine island of Palawan is considered a methane hydrate honey pot. The Philippines estimates that the Sampaguita Field within Recto Bank may also hold large deposits of natural gas equivalents in the form of methane hydrates.

The oil found in the Malampaya oil field off the Palawan coast already accounts for 40% of the energy needs of Luzon. The methane hydrates in Recto Bank will make the Philippines not only energy self-sufficient but can generate revenue from its export.

This is why Pres. Benigno Aquino Jr. warned China in his State of the Nation Address (SONA) in July 2011 that "if you set foot in Recto Bank, it will be as if you set foot on Recto Avenue. What's ours is ours."

Philippine Supreme Court Justice Antonio Carpio urged the Philippine government on May 20 to sue China for threatening war against the Philippines over the West Philippine Sea dispute.

Carpio wrote, "As a nation that under its Constitution has renounced war as an instrument of national policy, the Philippines' recourse is to bring China's threat of war to another UNCLOS arbitral tribunal, to secure an order directing China to comply with the ruling of the UNCLOS arbitral tribunal that declared the Reed Bank part of Philippine EEZ."

The UNCLOS tribunal at the Permanent Court of Arbitration in The Hague, Netherlands, ruled unanimously in July 2016 that China's expansive claim over the entire South China Sea was invalid but China has rejected the UN ruling.

Justice Carpio also urged the Philippine government to bring China's threat to go to war before the United Nations General Assembly by "sponsoring a resolution condemning China's threat of war against the Philippines and demanding that China comply with the ruling of the UNCLOS arbitral tribunal."

Filipinos in New York plan to rally in front of the United Nations on June 12 at noon to denounce China's threat of war against the Philippines.

"We are holding our rally fittingly on June 12 Philippine Independence Day because we want to show the world that while Filipinos fought for our independence from Spain in 1898, we will also fight for our independence from China in 2017," declared Loida Nicolas Lewis, national chair of the US Pinoys for Good Governance (USP4GG).

Independence Day protest rallies have been scheduled in front of the Philippine Embassy in Washington DC and in Philippine Consulates throughout the US simultaneously at noon on June 12.

If the Philippines does not protest China's threat of war, it will mean that the Philippines is surrendering its sovereignty to China. ."Acquiescence means the Philippines will lose forever its EEZ in the West Philippine Sea to China," Justice Carpio said.

(Celebrate June 12 Philippine Independence Day by asserting Philippine Inde-

pendence from China. Join the global protest rallies in front of your local Philippine consulates. Log on to USPGG.org for more information. Send comments to Rodel50@gmail.com or mail them to the Law Offices of Rodel Rodis at 2429 Ocean Avenue, San Francisco, CA 94127 or call 415.334.7800)

Ooooo

20
When We Are Fully Human
Fr. Shay Cullen
9 June 2017

The desire and longing to be a free and fully human is perhaps the deepest and strongest need of every person. It seems all creatures want freedom. Birds want freedom to fly from a cage, beasts to roam the land, monkeys to swing in the trees of the forest, fish to swim in the seas.

Humans want to be free to walk the earth without chains, guards, and fear in the power and custody of others. Personal freedom to speak the truth to power and political freedom are among the most important of all human freedoms.

What is it that makes us a human being I often ask the college students who come to study college-level psychology, social work and other subjects in their practicum internship at the Preda Foundation.

They come from many countries in Europe, from Canada, Japan, the Philippines and USA. I ask them to answer that basic question.

"Tell me in a few words, the attributes of the human person that set us apart from the other animals and makes us uniquely human." I ask that just to help us focus on whom and what we are. I am amazed as I am frequently met with embarrassed silence. What do you think makes us humans?

Well, the children at the Preda Home for Girls, ages 6 to 16 years, are pretty smart and they will raise their hands and speak up and they have true answers to the question. And that knowledge is what encourages and inspires them to be strong, resilient, brave and courageous in facing up and dealing with the most horrific thing that could happen to them- child rape and acts of sexual abuse.

Society has always unrated children, denied them their rights and dignity and used, enslaved and physically and sexually abused them as if they were not human. Many people do not see children, especially those not their own, as having rights especially the poor, skinny, malnourished and sickly children of the streets, those in prison as equally human. That's why so many are left to go hungry, uneducated and die of diseases before they reach ten years old.

In the Philippines, the Secretary of Justice justified the killing of the youth on mere suspicion of wrong-doing because they were "not humanity," he said. Therefore there could be no crime against humanity if they were summarily executed. I wonder if that argument would hold up in the International Criminal Court one day.

The amazing fact seems to be emerging of a Catholic country that has lost it

Christianity. Archbishop Socrates Villegas says many Filipino "Catholics" love the trappings and processions and outward devotions of Catholicism but he worries profoundly about what lies underneath the surface. They say they are Catholic but are they Christian is what the archbishop seems to ask.

In asking how Catholic they are, the outspoken Archbishop has said that they "declare faith, but agree that drug addicts should be shot... and many approve corruption in government." (See the full report on the Sunday Examiner 30 April 2017 and www.preda.org) The outspoken bishops are attacked online by thousands of critics. "When we speak, they want us muted, when we oppose they want us maimed, when we stand for life they want us dead," he said. Sad to say many bishops don't know what it is to be fully human and as a result they fail to act for justice and truth and gospel values.

Many have been silent so long they are now dumb. Fear is a powerful weapon. But the children, even when they are threatened even by death, they find the courage to speak out. When given the freedom, protection and empowerment they need they can speak out for justice and truth especially when they are the victims of injustice, rape and abuse.

The childhood of Anna Darling, 15, was taken away by a male pedophile known and approved to her mother and together they conspired to have Anna Darling made a sex slave with threats of killing her if she told. The fear kept her silent. She had nowhere to run to. Yet, the pain became unbearable and eventually she found a woman she trusted that listened to her and believed her and Anna Darling told her story.

She was rescued and after months in therapy at the Preda home with 42 other abused children, she began to heal. Soon she was ready and bravely asked to be able to testify against her abusers. The case is now in court and justice, we hope, will be done and be seen to be done.

Anna Darling discovered and believed that she has human rights, profound dignity, equality before God, that she was a child and the most important in the Kingdom of God and had civil and legal rights. She was empowered and overcame her fear. She learned too that her humanity is based on having reason and the ability to think for herself, to have knowledge of right and wrong and to have free will to choose the right over the wrong. She also found that she has the unique human ability to communicate and speak out the truth and to love others.

Anna Darling 15 used all five attributes of humanity to get justice. What a girl! If we could all be more reasonable, be actively thinking, knowing, choosing right over wrong, good over bad, truth over falsehood, speaking out and loving our neighbor what a different world we would live in.

shaycullen@gmail.com
www.preda.org.

ooooo

21
Vietnam: Uncle Sam's Newest Ally?

Perry Diaz
June 14, 2017, PerryScope

South Vietnamese general shoots suspected Viet Cong official in the head. (Ed Adams/AP).

Once enemies, the U.S. and Vietnam have become friends over the course of four decades. While it did not happen overnight, what transpired was a slow process of rapprochement between the two countries. It took two generations of Vietnamese and Americans to set aside the bitterness they both have on each other. Why not?

More than 58,000 American and 282,000 South Vietnamese soldiers were killed from 1955 to 1975. North Vietnam and the Viet Cong suffered 444,000 military casualties and 627,000 civilian deaths.

Last day of Vietnam War: South Vietnamese fleeing from the North Vietnamese try to get into a U.S. Marine helicopter on top of a tower at the U.S. Embassy in Saigon.

After the fall of Saigon, tens of thousands of South Vietnamese civilians and former soldiers fled the country. Known as "boat people," the refugees used boats of all sizes to escape the North Vietnamese communists. They migrated to other countries, in particular the nearby Philippines where the government resettled them. However, the U.S. was their country of choice; thus, the process of looking for sponsors began. American families opened their homes and welcomed them. Eventually, most of them were able to find jobs and own their homes. Over time, the Vietnamese immigrants were allowed to petition for family members provided that they have jobs and financial capability to put them up. By 2014, 1.3 million Vietnamese immigrants resided in the U.S.

Beyond the strong affinity displayed by the Vietnamese people toward their former enemies, government-to-government relations between the U.S. and Vietnam improved considerably.

Cultural and economic ties progressed at a pace that surpassed the most optimistic expectations.

Obama and Vietnam

President Barack Obama and his Vietnamese counterpart Truong Tan Sang shake hands at their meeting in Washington, DC.

On July 25, 2013, the historic meeting between President Barack Obama and his Vietnamese counterpart Truong Tan Sang in Washington, DC broke new ground in U.S.-Vietnam bilateral relations. Obama and Truong decided to form a U.S.-Vietnam Comprehensive Partnership, which underlined the principles of *"respect for the U.N. Charter, international law, and each other's political systems, independence, sovereignty, and territorial integrity."* The two leaders pledged that their countries would continue to cooperate on defense and security matters.

On May 23, 2016, Obama visited Hanoi and announced that the U.S. would fully lift a longstanding embargo on lethal arms sale to Vietnam, a decision that may have been precipitated by China's military build-up in the South China Sea (SCS). Obama said that the lifting of the arms embargo *"will ensure Vietnam has access to the equipment it needs to defend itself and removes a lingering vestige of the Cold War."*

Trump and Vietnam

President Donald Trump and Vietnamese Prime Minister Nguyen Xuan Phuc shake hands at their meeting in Washington, DC.

Recently, Vietnamese Prime Minister Nguyen Xuan Phuc visited President Donald J. Trump in the White House. His visit is significant because there have been perceptions that Vietnam was leaning to China, and the U.S. is veering away from the Indo-Asia-Pacific region. This caused many countries in the region – including Vietnam and the Philippines – to move closer to China. The leaders of the other eight ASEAN countries are adjusting their alignment as well. They're preparing themselves in the event that Trump would leave the region altogether.

But the U.S. visit of Nguyen has changed all that. Nguyen was the first ASEAN leader to visit Washington, DC since Trump was inaugurated president. With the meeting of Trump and Nguyen in the White House on May 31, it was evident that Trump is not reversing the course of

U.S. policy in the Indo-Asia-Pacific region. The "Pivot to Asia" that Obama started may have changed in name, but the objectives are the same: to protect U.S. interests in the Indo-Asia-Pacific region.

The meeting between the two leaders produced a joint statement to "Enhance the Comprehensive Partnership between the U.S. and Vietnam." Their joint statement reiterates that the *"United States is a 'Pacific power with widespread interests and commitments throughout the Asia Pacific.' It maintains all elements of the U.S.-Vietnam Comprehensive Partnership that was established during the Obama administration. It goes a step further, stating that President Trump and Prime Minister [Nguyen] Phuc are committed to making the partnership 'deeper, more substantive, and more effective.' For the first time the two former enemies stress at the summit level their 'pledge to strengthen cooperation in the fields of security and intelligence.' "*

Which makes one wonder: Is this just another diplomatic hyperbole or does it seem like it would lead to stronger defense and economic ties between the two countries? While a defense treaty would not be politically feasible at this time as it would certainly irk China and would also affect Vietnamese-Russian security relations, an arrangement similar to the U.S.-India Logistics Exchange Memorandum of Agreement (LEMOA) just might do the work. But while LEMOA might fall short of a "basing agreement," it gives the militaries of both countries access to each other's facilities for supplies and repair. It's a good start that could lead to a *de facto* – if not official – defense arrangement.

With this new U.S.-Vietnam Enhanced Comprehensive Partnership, the two countries would be able to deter China's aggressive behavior in the SCS; thus, protect Vietnam's EEZ from Chinese encroachment. Indeed, what is at stake is Vietnam's economic interest in the SCS.

Defense cooperation and the SCS issue were prominently addressed in the joint statement. Trump and Nguyen affirmed that the SCS is a "waterway of strategic significance." They also discussed the possibility of a visit to a Vietnamese port – Cam Ranh Bay — by a U.S. aircraft carrier and steps to further cooperation between their two naval forces.

Vietnam will never forget the Battle of the Paracel Islands in 1974 when China occupied the islands, which are claimed by Vietnam. Vietnam attempted to expel the Chinese Navy from the vicinity. A battle ensued and the Chinese forces prevailed. China established *de facto* control over the Paracels. However, Vietnam maintained her claim over the Paracels to this day.

A "first" in U.S.-Vietnam relations

China deploys giant oil rig in the waters near the Paracel Islands.

In 2014, China deployed her biggest oil rig into Vietnam's exclusive economic zone (EEZ). Vietnam then sent to the U.S. her number two man on the ruling Politburo, Executive Secretary of the Communist Party of Vietnam Dinh The Huynh. That was a "first" in U.S.-Vietnam relations.

Indeed, for the most part of the last two decades, the Philippines and Singapore led the rest of ASEAN in engaging the U.S. With the rift that Philippine President Rodrigo Duterte has with the U.S., the Philippines has cocooned herself into isolation. With the vacuum created by the Philippines, Vietnam would be more than willing to play a key role in engagement with the U.S.

U.S. donates six coastal patrol boats to Vietnam.

As a sign of closer U.S.-Vietnam military ties, the U.S. transferred six patrol boats to the Vietnam Coast Guard last May. The U.S. embassy released a statement, which said, *"The handover represented deepening cooperation to maritime law enforcement and humanitarian assistance in Vietnam's territorial waters and exclusive economic zone."*

U.S. Secretary of Defense James Mattis (5th L) poses for a picture with ASEAN defense leaders after a meeting on the sidelines of the 16th IISS Shangri-La Dialogue in Singapore, June 4, 2017.

At the recently concluded Shangri-La Dialogue in Singapore, U.S. Defense Secretary James Mattis said during his address to some 500 delegates: *"The US can't accept Chinese actions that impinge on the interests of the international community, undermining the rules-based order that has benefited all countries represented here today including, and especially, China."* He added that while conflict with China is not "inevitable," the two countries will engage in competition. And that's where Uncle Sam needs reliable allies to compete with China, which begs the question: Is Vietnam emerging as Uncle Sam's newest ally in the Indo-Asia-Pacific region?

(PerryDiaz@gmail.com)

Ooooo

22
Trump's Gunboat Diplomacy
Perry Diaz
June 7, 2017, PerryScope

Three U.S. supercarrier battle groups sail in formation.

In my column, *"China's gunboat diplomacy" (July 19, 2012)*, I wrote: " 'China frigate leaves shoal: [Malacañang] Palace happy,' said a huge electronic billboard, which I saw on the way to the Ninoy Aquino International Airport to catch a plane home last July 16, 2012. The news of a grounded guided missile Chinese frigate near Half Moon Shoal (Hasa-Hasa Shoal) in the Spratly archipelago, 69 miles west of Palawan, raised the tension level between the Philippines and China ever since the latter declared the entire West Philippine Sea (South China Sea) an extension of her territorial continental shelf in 2010. And China made it crystal clear that this vast body of water — rich in oil and natural gas deposits — is a 'core national *interest,' which in diplomatic parlance means 'non-negotiable.'*

"And to make sure that everybody — including the United States — knows that she is serious about her stand on the issue, China is building a naval force that would make her the dominant sea power in Asia-Pacific by 2020. And to let everybody know that she means business, she acquired an old aircraft carrier from Russia and retrofitted it with state-of-the-art technology and is now undergoing sea trials."

Floating airbases

New supercarrier USS Gerald R. Ford.

With 10 operational supercarriers and a new one — the USS Gerald R. Ford — joining the fleet in a few months, that means that the U.S. could deploy up to six carrier battle groups to cover the entire Indo-Asia-Pacific region. In addition to these supercarriers, the U.S. has nine amphibious assault ships that are more like aircraft carriers on a smaller scale.

Although China is way behind in her aircraft carrier-building program, she has now two carriers. The first one, a refurbished Cold War-era Russian carrier, is barely operational and the second – which was her first to build indigenously — is currently undergoing sea trials before she's commissioned for deployment. With a 10 to one ratio in favor of the U.S., the Chinese Navy wouldn't stand a chance against America's large fleet of supercarriers.

USS Langley (CV-1), the first aircraft carrier built in 1920.

Ever since the U.S. converted the collier USS Jupiter into an aircraft carrier — the USS Langley (CV-1) — in 1920, the U.S. became the world's dominant naval power because of her ability to deploy aircraft to these floating airbases at sea. Consequently, two more colliers were converted into aircraft carriers. After that, the U.S. built six brand-new aircraft carriers. By the time World War II erupted, America had the naval advantage no other world power had.

Big Stick ideology

Big Stick ideology.

With the capability to project air power in the high seas, the U.S. pursued her foreign policy objectives with what had come to be known as "gunboat diplomacy" or "Big Stick ideology." In other words, the conspicuous display of naval power anywhere in the world implies a direct threat of warfare, which forces another country to agree to terms America demands.

In World War II, the U.S. was able to defeat the Japanese naval forces in the Pacific because of the use of aircraft carriers. Had Japan destroyed America's aircraft carrier fleet based at Pearl Harbor in 1942, the outcome of the Pacific war might have been different. Fortunately, due to intelligence reports of an impending Japanese sneak attack on Pearl Harbor, the U.S. moved her entire aircraft carrier fleet out of harm's way into the open sea.

During the Cold War, the U.S. started building large nuclear-powered aircraft carriers that came to be known as "supercarriers." Following the new 100,000-ton Gerald R. Ford-class (CVN-78) of supercarriers, two others — the USS John F. Kennedy (CVN-79) and USS Enterprise (CVN-80) — are in various stages of construction.

Clinton's gunboat diplomacy

Taiwan Strait.

On July 21, 1995, the People's Republic of China (PRC) triggered what is called the 1995-1996 Taiwan Strait Crisis. That was when she fired a series of missile "tests" in the waters surrounding the Republic of China (ROC) – commonly known as Taiwan. It was believed that the first set of missiles was intended to send a "strong signal" to the Lee Teng-hui's government, who was perceived as moving the ROC's foreign policy away from the "One-China Policy." The second set of missiles was fired in early 1996. It was believed that it was intended to intimidate the Taiwanese voters in the run-up of the 1996 presidential election.

In March 1996, with the threat of PRC invasion, President Bill Clinton ordered the deployment of two supercarrier battle groups – the USS Nimitz and USS Independence – to the region. The Nimitz and the amphibious assault ship USS Belleau Wood daringly sailed through the Taiwan Strait, the narrow channel that separates the PRC from Taiwan. Unable to respond to the Nimitz's "provocation," the PRC realized then that she couldn't stop the U.S. from coming to the aid of Taiwan, and the PRC humiliatingly backed off.

Since then, the PRC embarked on a massive build-up of her naval forces. But today, she is still short of catching up to America's naval prowess. However, with more than a thousand land-based missiles deployed along China's coast facing Taiwan, China might be bold enough to respond next time the U.S. deploys a carrier battle group to the Taiwan Strait.

North Korea problem

North Korea launches multiple test missiles.

Recently, North Korea took a big step in the development of intercontinental ballistic missiles (ICBMs). She is also believed to possess of more than a dozen nuclear warheads that can be delivered by ICBMs, which would make the U.S. vulnerable to North Korean nuclear attack. It couldn't be ascertained if they're already operational. However, at the rate North Korea has been conducting missile tests, which seem to be successful, it would just be a matter of time before she becomes a threat to America's security.

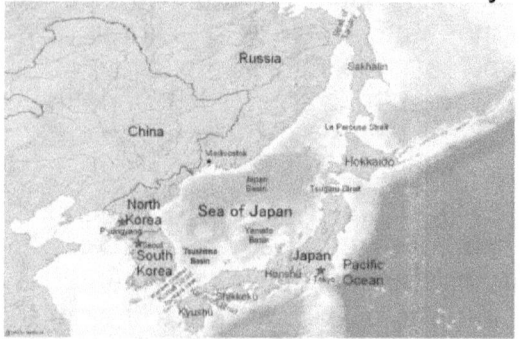

Sea of Japan.

In a move reminiscent of the 1995-1996 Taiwan Crisis, the Trump administration deployed two carrier battle groups – the USS

Ronald Reagan and USS Carl Vinson — to the Sea of Japan, which is within striking distance of North Korea.

In addition to the two battle groups, the USS Nimitz has been ordered to deploy to the Western Pacific to join the other two carrier battle groups. The deployment of Nimitz marks a rare situation, when a total of three carrier battle groups are simultaneously deployed in one region. Some analysts say that the Nimitz's deployment might be a "special contingency plan." With four to five guided missile cruisers and destroyers and one or two nuclear attack submarines accompanying each supercarrier, the large assemblage of naval assets in a theater of operations has never been bigger since the end of World War II.

There has been a lot of speculation about what's in President Donald Trump's mind when he allowed three carrier battle groups to converge in waters near North Korea. In a recent telephone conversation between Philippine President Rodrigo Duterte, Trump told Duterte: *"We have two submarines — the best in the world. We have two nuclear submarines, not that we want to use them at all."* In response to news report of their conversation, North Korean officials said that their country was ready for nuclear attacks in the event of "U.S. military aggression."

With the White House loaded with retired military generals whom Trump has given a lot of latitude to decide what military action to take when the need arises, there are two ways this situation could lead to. One would be to use the template of Clinton's "gunboat diplomacy" during the 1995-1996 Taiwan Strait Crisis that could compel North Korea to back off and sue for peace. If that is going to happen, then Trump's "gunboat diplomacy" works. However, if North Korea fights back with a nuclear attack on South Korea, then all hell breaks loose!

(PerryDiaz@gmail.com)

ooooo